CREMATION

PAUL E. IRION

Fortress Press, Philadelphia

Preface

CREMATION is an ancient practice, but there seems to be recurrent need for a new perspective on it. Since World War II in England the percentage of deaths in which cremation was employed to dispose of the body has risen from seven per cent to 46.9 per cent. During the same period in the United States the percentage of cremations has been comparatively static, still representing slightly less than four per cent of the total number of deaths annually. The situation is that large numbers of our people have given little serious thought to this means for disposing of the bodies of the dead.

There appear to be a number of reasons behind the failure of this process to gain favor with the American people as it has done in England. These reasons merit very brief discussion.

There is in our American culture a pervasive avoidance of death and anything associated with it. Thus there is reluctance on the part of many to give thoughtful consideration to the meaning of funerary practices or to plan in advance just how the funeral could be most helpful to them in bereavement. They much prefer to ignore the possibility of personal bereavement, or they wait until a death occurs in the family and then conform uncritically and unreflectively to existing patterns.

A second reason is the resistance to major innovation in the sacred rituals and secular customs surrounding death. Cremation in the United States is largely practiced in urban centers and predominantly on the West Coast. This means that for a sizable number of the communities of the nation cremation is rarely or occasionally employed. It still is for many an innovation, and it may not even be accorded serious consideration in funeral planning. Faced with urgent decisions, most families then do not depart far from familiar practices.

Yet another reason is an emotional reaction against the thought of burning the dead. The rapid destruction of the body or mental pictures of the process deter some persons from giving consideration to cremation. The popular understanding of the processes of preparing a dead body leads to the assumption that the body remains intact for a long period, and there is not then the same strong repugnance to the slower, but equally destructive, deterioration of the body in the grave.

Religious resistance has been still another factor hindering acceptance of cremation on a broader scale. Most of the Judeo-Christian faith groups have in the past opposed or do presently oppose cremation. Even when official ecclesiastical positions regarding cremation have been modified, popular reluctance to support the practice has often continued. Although many of the commonly voiced reasons for religious opposition are not a part of the teaching of any church or synagogue, the layman often holds tenaciously to them.

Then too, cremation has not made rapid strides in America because factors of particular urgency are not pressing in our nation. Only in a few megalopolitan areas is economy of land usage the urgent concern it is in England or Japan. In those nations the crucial need for land formerly intended for burial ground has lent emphasis to the need to use a more effective and less space-consuming means for dealing with the bodies of the dead.

Finally, a good bit of the public indifference to cremation results from sheer lack of information. Many people have neither made nor taken the opportunity to learn about cremation. They have never had occasion to visit a crematorium. They have not read even the very limited literature on the subject. Their personal contacts with it have been so narrow that they have little knowledge of what the process involves and have thought little about its implications.

The purpose of this book is three-fold. It is an effort to encourage discussion of cremation, to provide information about it and its implications and to foster a climate in community and church in which individuals and families will have a free choice in their selection of funerary practices.

Only against a background of thoughtful discussion can this purpose be accomplished. There is need for people to gain understanding of the meaning and the function of various funerary practices. Instead of being based on personal prejudice or uninformed preference, such understanding should be grounded in our best knowledge of the needs of the bereaved and of the place of our customs and practices in meeting those needs. Families need to be encouraged to talk over their own points of view and to establish tentative plans for the ways in which they will seek to meet the needs of members of the family when death comes near.

This kind of discussion requires information. One needs to know as much as possible about what is involved in cremation: its history, the process itself, its psychological, theological and social implications. One must view critically and dispassionately the arguments which have been advanced both for and against cremation.

The goal of information and discussion is to make free choice possible. Freedom is only as wide as the scope of the options available. Hopefully individuals and families, by having a number of possibilities open to them, will reach decisions that prove to be helpful to them when they face the crisis of bereavement.

This book should not be seen as a special pleading in favor of cremation. I have endeavored to be as objective as possible and to provide data for impartial study of the subject.

Thus the reader is not being challenged unconditionally to accept cremation but is rather asked to consider carefully its meaning and its implications and then to formulate his own stance. To assist in this formulation an appendix contains a self-study questionnaire by which one can seek to clarify his own attitudes on the subject.

PAUL IRION
Lancaster, Pa.
September, 1966

Contents

1

Cremation Historically Reviewed

CREMATION is a way of disposing of the body of one who has died. Virtually every known culture has surrounded the event of death with a structure of ritual and practice designed to do several things: to make some disposition of the body of the dead, to convey in some way the meanings given to life and death by the group, to support surviving members of the clan or family and to aid their adjustment to life without the one who has died. These functions become interwoven as customs and rituals develop. So even though we are dealing with cremation, a mode of disposing of the body of the deceased, we are also involved with other elements of funerary practice.

There has always been considerable interest in the history of various funeral customs. Cultural anthropologists and historians have maintained a lively professional concern for understanding how cultures met the crisis of death. Nonprofessionals have shared this interest, fascinated as tourists and sightseers, readers and students, with the tombs and monuments, pyramids and mummified bodies which show something of ways in which other peoples and other generations dealt with their dead.

Historically one can observe a great many modes of disposing of the body of one who has died. Some of these seem strange and barbaric to us. Some are found in many cultures, although there is no distinctly universal form of disposing of a dead body. Possibly the earliest form was cave burial. Burial in the earth in a man-made grave, barrow or cairn is another ancient form. Burning of the body has also been widely practiced since very early times. Less common and less well-known modes of disposition are water burial, simple exposure to the elements, preservation of the body in a quasi-dwelling and cannibalism.

So often funerary customs seem to be judged on the basis of age and point of origin. The superficial assumption has frequently been made that the older something is, the better it is. Or it has been supposed that if something has its origin outside of one's own culture, it is inferior and unusable.

Cremation, although it is found even in prehistoric times, is in all probability not the oldest form of disposition. It must be pointed out that, although it has had a prominent place in many other cultures, in its modern form it did not become a part of what we call Western culture until late in the nineteenth century.

From a very brief overview of cremation as it has been practiced since the dawn of history we need to seek answers to several questions: Why has this particular mode been used? How does it relate to the meanings of life and death? What does it accomplish for the mourners? Of course, in many instances we shall not possess sufficient evidence to give complete answers, but at least we can point a direction.

CREMATION IN PREHISTORIC TIMES

Archeological evidence points to the origin of cremation during the Stone Age in eastern Europe or the Near East. It spread across northern Europe during the late Stone Age and probably came to the British Isles by invasion from Brittany in the early Bronze Age. Its extension into the Iberian Peninsula late in the Bronze Age would give some indication of the remoteness of its source.

The beginnings of cremation are obscure. Perhaps Charles Lamb's *A Dissertation upon Roast Pig* could be paralleled here. James[1] suggests that the first cremations may well have been accidental. There is evidence that in early prehistoric times, when recognizable cults of the dead already existed, fire was associated with funerary ritual. Sometimes fire was used as a means for drying and preserving the body. Sometimes, the presence of charred animal bones in burial caves suggests, the fire may have been part of preparation for a funeral feast or of a sacrificial ritual. In other instances, the fire may have been part of a purification ceremony. It is conjectured that the use of fire in funerals probably existed before the general adoption of cremation. It is conceivable that the body could have been burned accidentally by such funerary fires. The discovery of partially burned bodies in prehistoric graves may be the result of such accidental cremations.

There is little question among archeologists, however, that many other prehistoric cremations were intentional.

---

[1] E. O. James, *Prehistoric Religion* (London: Thames & Hudson, 1957), p. 99.

This is seen in the reasonably standardized ways in which deliberate attention was given to the collection and disposition of the charred bones of the corpse. These remains are found because incineration was not complete since only open fires were available. In the valleys of the Dniester and Dnieper Rivers archeological evidence has been discovered of special sites where cremations were performed by Slavic tribes in the late Stone Age.[2] Excavations have also discovered evidence in widespread sections of Europe that the remains of the cremated body were buried. Sometimes the bones were just heaped up and covered with earth or stones. In many other instances, where people had learned to make pottery, the charred bones were interred in urns of distinctive design.

> On the continent, cremation cemeteries in the form of urn fields became general at this time (i.e. from the Middle Bronze Age to the Early Iron Age, from about 1500 to 800 B.C.) first in Hungary and Northern Italy, and then extending from Western Asia Minor throughout Western, Central and Northern Europe to Ireland. Genuine cremation with the ashes deposited in urns which were buried in large cemeteries now was so widely adopted that it marks a definite transition in the cult of the dead . . .[3]

There is little question that cave and earth burial were earlier forms of disposition than cremation. The fact that many prehistoric burial grounds contain both burned and unburned bodies indicates that both forms of disposition were practiced by the same peoples. One might also suppose that since deliberate burial of the burned bodies was made, cremation was an element

[2] "Death and Disposal of the Dead," *Encyclopedia of Religion and Ethics,* ed. James Hastings, IV (1912), 508.

[3] James, *op. cit.,* p. 101.

being added to the already existing pattern of burial. Cremation did become general practice in pre-Christian Europe, but it apparently never did completely replace burial.

CREMATION IN THE ANCIENT WORLD

The spread of cremation through the ancient world was rather general. Only a few cultures resisted the practice. The Egyptians, of course, developed various processes for preserving the body by embalming. The Chinese consistently buried their dead and the Jews gradually changed from cave and sepulchre to earth burial. The Persians continued their practice of exposure to scavenger birds.

The Babylonians practiced both cremation and burial. Near Lagash two ancient crematoriums have been excavated. The corpses were wrapped in combustible material and encased in clay. Then they were placed on a brick platform and enclosed in a funeral pyre. The ashes were collected and placed in jars and accompanied with grave goods, indicating some belief in the continuing presence of the spirit of the deceased.[4]

The Greeks

It is believed that the practice of cremation entered ancient Greece from the North around 1000 B.C., replacing in part the elaborate burial customs of the Mycenaean culture. Its use increased until it became the prevalent form of disposition by the time of the Homeric period. Several explanations have been offered for the establishment of cremation as the popular mode of disposal. As knowledge increased, disposition of the dead was regulated to prevent health menace. Plato urged that burials not be made in fields under cultivation, and rules prohibiting burials near inhabited

[4] *Encyclopedia of Religion and Ethics,* IV, 444–46.

buildings were established. At the time of Pericles a plague resulted in many deaths, and the use of cremation as a sanitary measure was encouraged.

The Homeric literature, supported by Pliny, indicates that cremation was used to dispose of the bodies of Greek soldiers who died in battle in foreign lands to prevent disinterment and desecration of the bodies by the enemy after the army withdrew. The ashes of the fallen soldiers were taken back to their homeland for ceremonial entombment. The fact that the ashes of the cremated were in most instances buried would appear to indicate that cremation was an addition to the older custom of burial.

Even though the practice became commonly used, it still was not universal. Because it was fairly elaborate, it was costly and could not be adopted by the poorer people. It is also interesting to note that the right to be cremated was denied to suicides, infants who did not yet have teeth, and persons struck by lightning and thus assumed to be in disfavor with the gods. This suggests that cremation was assumed to affect the dead differently than burial.

This may well be due to the philosophical system upon which Greek life was based. The dualistic assumptions of this system made the obvious separation of soul from body a very desirable thing. Death and the dissolution of the body provided the means for the emancipation of the soul. This objective combined with the assertion of Heraclitus that fire was the underlying principle for all existence. Fire symbolized the purification and release of the soul and the unification of the body with its original elements.

This practice did not imply a total disparagement of the material body, because the ashes were collected in urns. At times grave goods such as coins and artifacts were placed with or near the ashes. There is evidence that at other times the possessions of the deceased were burned along with him.

The Romans

The ancient Romans quite possibly received the custom of cremation through the Greeks. Its introduction has been dated by some as the sixth century B.C. Other authors present cremation as an early practice. Virgil mentions it as being in use before the foundation of Rome and Ovid says that the body of Remus was cremated. The Laws of the Twelve Tables in the middle of the fifth century B.C. prohibit both burial and burning of bodies within the city, showing that both practices were then in use. An unusual combination of the two customs is seen in the practice of *os resectum* in which a member, usually part of a finger, was cut off from the corpse before cremation. The funeral rites were observed with this severed member as a focus after the rest of the body had been cremated.[5] The *os resectum* was then buried, thus maintaining overtones of interment in cremation practices.

During the Republic and at the time of the Empire cremation was widely practiced in Rome and its provinces. For example, the Emperor Severus was cremated in York in 217 A.D. and his ashes were returned to Rome.[6]

As in Greece, cremation was especially used for the wealthier people. The poorer people may have been cremated with much smaller pyres or on communal pyres and without the addition of expensive pitch or oil to complete the incineration. "To call a man's ancestor

[5] Alfred C. Rush, *Death and Burial in Christian Antiquity* (Washington: The Catholic University of America Press, 1941), p. 241.

[6] C. J. Polson, R. P. Brittain, T. K. Marshall, *The Disposal of the Dead* (New York: Philosophical Library, 1953), p. 84.

'half burned' was a well-understood insult, involving, by implication, reference to an insufficient funeral pile prepared for a great number of corpses [of the poor]."[7] Burial was commonly used for the very poor and for children.

There apparently was some relationship between the growing practice of cremation and beliefs about an afterlife. Cremation would not be practiced by those who assumed that the life of the body was going to continue very similar to present existence. They would endeavor to keep the body intact. Those who, on the other hand, thought of the soul alone continuing life after death would seek means for releasing it from its bodily matrix. Several Roman practices imply this understanding. According to one custom, as the funeral pyre burned, a bird was released to symbolize the upward flight of the spirit.[8] Another custom involved the assumption that the spirit of the deceased, upon release in cremation, would be in contact with the spirits of others who had died earlier. So attempts were made to communicate with the dead through him. "Diodorus, Caesar's contemporary, says 'At the burial of the dead, some cast letters addressed to their departed relatives upon the funeral pile, under the belief that the dead will read them.' Mela confirms this, saying 'Business accounts and payments of debts were passed on to the next world.' "[9]

The Romans preserved the ashes in cinerary urns, often elaborately decorated. Extensive columbariums in which the urns were placed have been discovered.

[7] Arnold Wilson and Hermann Levy, *Burial Reforms and Funeral Costs* (London: Oxford University Press, 1938), p. 6.

[8] *Encyclopedia of Religion and Ethics,* IV, 506.

[9] W. H. F. Basevi, *The Burial of the Dead* (London: George Routledge & Sons, 1920), pp. 113–14.

The Jews

In contrast to the Greeks and the Romans, the ancient Jewish people rarely employed cremation. It always remained the rare exception rather than the rule. The Old Testament records several instances of cremation. When Saul and his sons died in battle, their bodies were burned by the men of Jabesh Gilead (I Sam. 31: 12–13) after the Philistines had mutilated and displayed them. Then they buried the bones. This exceptional disposition was probably to prevent further ignominious treatment of the bodies. A later parallel account of the death of Saul (I Chron. 10:12) omits reference to the cremation, indicating perhaps reluctance to acknowledge cremation as a legitimate form of disposition.

There is reference to burning bodies at Tophet (Jer. 7:31) but it is not clear whether it refers to cremation or to human sacrifice. In either case it is not regarded with approval. Reference is made to cremation of ancient kings of Judah (II Chron. 16:14, 21:19).

Hebrew sentiment against cremation is seen in references which reserve burning for the bodies of animals and criminals (cf. Josh. 7:15, 25). Earth burial or sepulture always remained standard practice.

The Christians

The early Christians first tended to adapt local custom to their practices. Christians in Jewish communities retained sepulture or burial. Coptic Christians in Egypt retained the practice of mummification. But the Roman practice of cremation and burying the *os resectum* apparently was not followed by the Christians.

No clear reason for this resistance to cremation is apparent. Various suggestions have been made. Preference for inhumation may have been a simple following of the precedent of Jesus' burial in the tomb of Joseph of

Arimathea according to the custom of the Jewish people. Perhaps the expectation of "rising with Christ" produced a desire to imitate the mode of his burial.

Emphasis upon the Christian hope for the resurrection may also have caused the preference for burial over cremation. Although Christians did not suppose that destruction of the body by fire would preclude resurrection, the symbolism of the body at rest in the grave may have been a significant context for belief in the resurrection. The enemies of Christianity assumed that preservation of the body was necessary to resurrection for the Christian and in times of persecution took extreme steps to prevent burial or to devise means of execution which would destroy the body as an entity. Eusebius described a persecution in Lyon in 177 A.D. in this way:

> After torture and execution the bodies of the martyrs were guarded by soldiers, so that their friends could not bury them. Finally after some days the bodies were burned and reduced to ashes and swept into the Rhone "so that no trace of them might appear on the earth." And this they did as if able to conquer God, and prevent their new birth; "that," as they said, "they may have no hope of a resurrection."[10]

The position of the early church is further described in a dialog of Minucius Felix, the *Octavius*. In this debate between Caecilius, a pagan, and Octavius, a Christian, cremation is discussed.

> After casting aspersions on the belief in the resurrection and the promise of a happy eternity with which the Christians delude themselves, Caecilius says: "Hence it is easy to understand why they curse our funeral pyres and condemn cremation, just as if everybody, although withdrawn from the flames, were not reduced to dust as the years roll

[10] *The Church History of Eusebius*, Bk. V, chap. 1.

on. . . ." In his reply, Octavius . . . states: "We are not, as you imagine, afraid of any injury from the manner of burial, but we practice the older and better practice of interment."[11]

There was in the Christian view generally a resistance to the disparagement of the material world, including the physical body, which was part of the prevailing dualism of the time. The human body was seen as the work of the Creator and was regarded as worthy of respect. Origen writes, "It is the reasonable soul which we honor, and we commit its bodily organs with due honors to the grave."[12] Tertullian was even more explicit: "There is, however, another way of accounting for this pious treatment [of resisting cremation], not as if it meant to favor the relics of the soul, but as if it would avert cruelty even in regard to the body; since being human, it certainly does not deserve to have *such a punishment* [author's italics] inflicted upon it."[13] Such statements from the fathers in the early church show the kind of judgment that was made against cremation and in favor of burial. No reasons are given against cremation on the basis of New Testament teachings or dogma, but cremation is identified as pagan and resisted as not showing proper regard for the body of the Christian. Thus it would appear that early Christian resistance to cremation was stimulated more by strong reaction against the pagan protagonists of cremation than by reasons against the practice inherent in the Christian faith. The mode of burial became one of the significant marks that distinguished the Christian from the pagan in these centuries.

After the legalization of Christianity under Constantine and the expansion of the church's influence the practice

11 Rush, *op. cit.*, p. 236.
12 Origen, *Contra Celsum*, VIII, 30.
13 Tertullian, *De Anima*, 51.

11

of burial rather than cremation grew more prevalent. Laws were passed under the Emperor Theodosius in 381 A.D. regulating burial, particularly forbidding burial in the city of Rome and other cities. The practice of burying Christians within the walls of their churches was discontinued, with some exceptions made for the wealthy or the pre-eminent. By the fifth century the practice of burial superseded cremation in the Christian world.

CREMATION IN THE EAST

Many Asian cultures have practiced cremation as a traditional form of disposition of the dead. A notable exception has been the Chinese. Traditionally the Chinese have sought to preserve the body, and burial has commended itself as the best means to this end. There are instances in Chinese history in which cremation was practiced, but it probably grew out of foreign domination.

In Tibet cremation is practiced where fuel is available. In some of the bleak mountainous areas it is impractical. The high lamas have customarily been cremated. A unique feature of Tibetan cremation is the collection and grinding of the ashes which are cast into medallions. The medallions are then placed in suitable niches as memorials.

In Japan the Shinto religion has customarily used earth burial, although cremation has sometimes been practiced and the Shinto burial ritual used when the ashes were interred. The Zen and Tendai Buddhists permit either burial or cremation. Although as late as 1875 cremation was officially forbidden, in modern Japan it is an extremely common occurrence. In urban areas lack of space for burial has caused cremation to be made mandatory.

In Thailand it is the practice to preserve the body for a time by embalming and then to cremate it with elaborate ritual. Royalty are sometimes preserved in a temple for six months or a year before cremation. The time period is normally determined by the social rank of the individual. Poorer families sometimes do not have the means to purchase fuel for cremation at the time of death and will bury the body, exhuming it later for cremation when this is possible.

Cremation began in India as early as the second millennium B.C. according to James.[14] It probably supplanted earth burial because the ashes of the cremated were buried. In the Rig-Veda there is reference in a funeral hymn invoking the fire god to speed the deceased on his way to the abode of the dead without consuming him.[15]

> Among the Aryans the idea that fire was the only medium by which sacrifice could reach the gods may have led to introduction of the process of cremation after the belief in an abode in the sky where the soul joined the *petri,* the sainted dead, had become firmly established.[16]

The religious and philosophical dimensions of Indian thought imply that fire resolves the body into its basic elements of fire, water, earth and air, while at the same time purifying the spirit in preparation for its reincarnation. Various sects and tribes take steps in the ritual to prevent the released spirit from returning to the scenes of his former existence. Some take care, because of threatened reprisals, to perform the ritual correctly in order to give the spirit repose. Some seek to confuse

[14] James, *op. cit.,* p. 248.
[15] *Ibid.*
[16] *Encyclopedia of Religion and Ethics,* IV, 483.

the spirit so that he will lose his way back to his home village.[17]

There are some exceptions to the practice of cremation. The age of the deceased often determines the mode of disposition. Children who die are usually buried, sometimes at the threshold of their home. It is believed that burial makes it possible for them to be reborn, to begin life again. Eliade links this form of burial to a return to the womb of the Earth Mother.[18] Certain ascetics are also buried and among the Gurkhas burial is often given to those who die with infectious diseases. In some sections of South India married persons are cremated and those who die unmarried are buried.

Until its prohibition in 1829 the custom of *suttee*, Hindu wife-immolation, was practiced. The widow was required to jump into her husband's pyre. It was not simply an act of loyalty or devotion but had an economic base. It was a custom designed to preserve the widow's dowry and her husband's property for his family by removing her as the heiress.

Cremation in India is carried out with a funeral pyre constructed of special wood according to prescribed plans. If possible, fats and oils are added to aid the burning. The poor are often unable to make suitable pyres, and in some areas a shortage of wood is a problem, so that cremation is sometimes very incomplete.

In some sects the ashes or partly cremated body is put into the Ganges or another sacred river. In other parts of India the bones are collected and buried in an urn.

[17] David Mandelbaum, "Social Uses of Funeral Rites," in *The Meaning of Death*, ed. Herman Feifel (New York: McGraw-Hill Book Co., 1959), pp. 189–217. Cf. Effie Bendann, *Death Customs: An Analytical Study of Burial Rites* (New York: Alfred A. Knopf, 1920), pp. 46–47.

[18] Mircea Eliade, *Patterns in Comparative Religion*, trans. Rosemary Sheed (New York: Sheed & Ward, 1958), p. 250.

CREMATION IN THE WESTERN WORLD

As has already been indicated, cremation had become a generally accepted practice in the Western world until the advance of Christianity. The influence of the Christian church spread across the Roman Empire and its successors from the fourth century on. Wherever its influence was felt the practice of earth burial replaced cremation.

A variety of explanations have been offered for this pervasive change in firmly established custom. It was brought about by a massive change in public opinion in most instances rather than by a direct proscription of cremation.

The Christian influence, with its expressed preference for burial, made itself felt generally upon Roman culture after the time of Constantine. When the decline of the Empire brought rapid changes to the social order, traditions and practices became so fluid that revision of customs was made easier. It is even possible that the facilities for cremation were not maintained as the Empire dissolved.[19]

The Christian resistance to cremation was further intensified because the practice was associated with pagan sacrifice, both in form and in some of its implications in pagan cultures. As the conversion of Europe proceeded and the influence of the church became stronger, concerted efforts were made to root out vestiges of pagan practice. Cremation was widely regarded as one of these. In 789 Charlemagne proclaimed punishment by death for those who cremated "following the rites of pagans."

It has also been theorized that the change from cremation to burial was not religiously motivated but grew out of the desire of the wealthy to have expensive tombs and sarcophagi and because of the high cost and un-

[19] Polson, *et al., op. cit.*, p. 85.

availability of fuel for cremation.[20] This reasoning is not fully convincing because cremation was replaced by burial even when Christianity went into northern Europe which had ample fuel and because expensive memorials can be constructed as depositories for cremated remains as easily as for the body.

The resistance to cremation in Christian Europe was effective for 1500 years. A few exceptions were made, permitting cremation in times of plague or after major battles when it was not possible to dispose of all the dead by burial. Such exceptions were infrequent.

> Once in the course of the Middle Ages did there seem to be on the part of some a retrogression to the pagan ideals, and as a consequence Boniface VIII on 21 February 1300, in the sixth year of his pontificate, promulgated a law which was in substance as follows: They were *ipso facto* excommunicated who disembowelled bodies of the dead or inhumanely boiled them to separate the flesh from the bones, with a view to transportation for burial in their native land. He speaks of it as an abomination in the sight of God and horrifying to the minds of the faithful, decreeing that thereafter, such bodies are rather to be conveyed whole to the spot chosen or buried at the place of death until, in the course of nature, the bones can be removed for burial elsewhere.[21]

The following incident will show further how much cremation was derogated as a proper means for disposing of the bodies of the faithful. The Council of Constance, to show its disdain for the condemned heretic John Wycliffe, ordered in 1428 (forty-four years after his death) that his body should be dug up and cremated and the ashes thrown into a river.

In Scandinavia cremation had been practiced at least

[20] Rush, *op. cit.*, p. 253.
[21] "Cremation," *The Catholic Encyclopedia*, IV (1908), 482.

as early as the Bronze Age. A distinctive form of cremation in Nordic culture was the fire ship. The funeral pyre was built on a ship which was set ablaze and sent out to sea. An earlier form appears to have been burial in a grave ship. Cremation persisted in Scandinavia until the Christianization of northern Europe after the tenth century A.D. Then it was gradually and completely replaced by earth burial.

In 1658 a book of burial practices was written by Sir Thomas Browne.[22] He included a discussion of cremation and described Roman cinerary urns. This appears to be the first objective treatment of the subject in many centuries.

Occasional cremations took place in various parts of Europe. There is a record that in 1710 a Mrs. John Pratt, wife of the Treasurer of Ireland, directed that her body should be cremated because of the atrocious condition of graveyards. Her plan evoked considerable public outcry. In 1797 the French Assembly under the Directory gave serious consideration to legalizing cremation but no action resulted. In 1822 the English poet Shelley and a companion were drowned in the Mediterranean near Leghorn. According to Tuscan quarantine law they were cremated as protection against plague. Again public attention was attracted to this means of disposition.

THE MODERN CREMATION MOVEMENT

In the second half of the nineteenth century new interest in cremation developed in Italy, Germany, England and the United States. The major thrust began in Italy.

Italy

The modern support for cremation involved not only renewed interest in the ancient practice but also de-

[22] *Hydriotaphia or Urn Burial.*

velopment of a new method. Until this time cremations had usually been accomplished with a funeral pyre. In 1869–72 a number of experiments were made independently by Professors Polli, Gorini and Brunetti, developing furnaces for the purpose of effective cremation. Reports of the construction of gas or coal cremation furnaces were published in Italy in 1872 by those scientists. Professor Brunetti exhibited a model of his furnace and some cremated remains at the Vienna Exposition in 1873, attracting a good deal of public attention.

Designing such apparatus was no easy task. Some of the earlier experimental models were not fully satisfactory because they did not provide sufficient heat to accomplish their purpose efficiently and inexpensively. New designs were made by Siemens in Germany which made possible virtually total incineration of the body quickly, efficiently and inexpensively, without any pollution of the atmosphere.

Cremation had been written about and discussed in various health congresses since 1852. A number of eminent Italian scientists and physicians became ardent supporters of the process. At international health congresses in Florence and Rome resolutions in favor of legislation permitting cremation were endorsed. The Italian government responded favorably to these proposals and legalized cremation. In 1876, delayed several years by the resistance of municipal officials, the practice was instituted in Milan where a society was organized to operate a crematorium.

Cremation was practiced also in Genoa and Rome and other cities of Italy, although it was not accepted widely in the southern portion of the country. Erichsen reports the *early* response of the Roman Catholic church to the practice:

The Italian clergy opposed incineration but very little. In the capital of Lombardy a distinguished prelate even declared that the burning of the dead is in no wise contradictory to the dogma of the church; and here one also can witness how priests accompany the body to be incinerated to the *Tempio Crematorio,* where they say a last prayer, indeed proof of tolerance and genuine Christianity.[23]

Germany

In Germany there was at the same time growing support for cremation. It was closely related to rising political liberalism under sponsorship of J. Grimm and Rudolph Virchow. The basis of the *Freidenker* philosophy was a materialistic understanding of the human body through biological research. There were also strong antitheological and anti-ecclesiastical dimensions to this position because of resistance in the church to cremation. The first German crematorium was established in Gotha, in central Germany, in 1878.

Cremation gained approval slowly in northern Germany. In 1855 it had been proposed in Prussia that cremation be legalized. This brought strong opposition, particularly from the churches. It took twenty years for a bill legalizing cremation to be voted by the Diet in Prussia, but it finally passed by two votes in 1911. In the Roman Catholic southern parts of Germany cremation still was not permitted.

England

In England the modern cremation movement was inspired by Sir Henry Thompson, surgeon to Queen Victoria. He shared the growing concern of many leaders for the dangers to public health arising out of the condition of English graveyards. The Report of the

[23] Hugo Erichsen, *The Cremation of the Dead* (Detroit: D. O. Haynes & Co., 1887), pp. 49–50.

Select Committee in 1842 had publicized the deplorable conditions of cemeteries and had inspired some burial legislation which sought to reduce the dangers to health of shallow burials in overcrowded graveyards in a rapidly urbanizing country. The London Commission of 1849 produced a similar report based on the findings of eminent professors of medicine and science. One solution proposed to meet the growing problem was cremation.

Sir Henry attended the Vienna Exposition in 1873 and saw the exhibit of Brunetti's cremation furnace. In January of 1874 he published an article favoring cremation in *The Contemporary Review,* beginning an extended literary debate with opposition that developed immediately both from the Church of England and from the public. Some of the issues in the controversy concerned water pollution from graveyards, removal of cemeteries from urban areas, the waste of land devoted to cemeteries rather than to parks and playing fields.

Those who allied themselves with Thompson's cause formed a Cremation Society of England in 1874. Many of these early proponents were political liberals and socialists and people without professed religious commitment.

> It was agreed that upon payment of an annual subscription membership of the Cremation Society was open to any person who was prepared to make the following declaration: "We disapprove the present custom of burying the dead, and desire to substitute some mode which shall rapidly resolve the body into its component elements by a process which cannot offend the living, and shall render the remains absolutely innocuous. Until some better method is devised, we desire to adopt that usually known as cremation."[24]

[24] C. J. Polson, *et al., op. cit.,* p. 87

By 1878 the society had sufficient funds to construct a crematorium. The first plan of the society was to construct its crematorium in conjunction with an existing cemetery in London. However, the Bishop of Rochester, who had jurisdiction over the cemetery, refused the permission of the Anglican church. So the society erected the crematorium at Woking, using a furnace built by Professor Gorini.

However, legal permission for cremation to take place could not be obtained. The Home Secretary, who had charge of matters dealing with public health and safety, was opposed to cremation. Sir Henry was required to promise that there would be no cremations without the approval of the Home Secretary. Because this approval was not given, the situation reached an impasse. So the society changed its purpose to public education regarding the advantages of cremation.

Two events took place several years later which helped to break the deadlock. In 1882 a Captain Hanham requested permission from the Home Secretary for the society to cremate his wife and his mother. Permission was denied. Captain Hanham then had a crematorium built on his own estate and proceeded with the cremations. When he died in 1883, he was also cremated there. In spite of the lack of official approval the authorities did not act against these cremations.

In 1883 a Dr. Price cremated the body of an infant son in a field after refusing an inquest and registration of the death. Police extinguished the fire, recovered the body and held an autopsy which showed death from natural causes. Dr. Price was arrested and tried for cremating without permission in order to avoid inquest. In 1884 he was acquitted. This verdict opened the way for cremation by affirming that it was a legal procedure, so long as it did not constitute a nuisance to others. The society now considered itself free to begin cremations at Woking. It expressed its sense of legal responsibility by recognizing the potential danger of destroying evidence of foul play by cremating the body of the victim without autopsy. So the society voluntarily accepted procedures even more stringent than those normally involved in certifying cause of death. Even to the present time in England the approval of two independent medical examiners and a medical referee is required before cremation can be authorized.

Debate began in Parliament to make cremation explicitly legal. This debate drew a great deal of public attention to the issue and press coverage of the debate helped to clarify the real and specious issues in the controversy. However, for eighteen years cremation was not illegal, but there was no law expressly permitting it. In 1902 the first cremation act was passed. This law provided for the necessary assent before death of the person to be cremated and codified the protections against destruction of evidence of cause of death. This act was revised in 1930 and in 1952.

The society had proceeded with cremations at Woking on the basis of the Price verdict. The first cremation was in 1885. Within six years Sir Henry Thompson reported 177 cremations at Woking. At first there was violent opposition from the public and the church. On some occasions police were required to keep the peace.

In 1901 the city of Hull established a municipal crematorium, beginning a trend of municipal or regional ownership that has predominated in England.

Following World War II it became apparent that England had to take land usage very seriously. Urban growth reduced the land available for public use. Extensions of cemeteries appeared to many to be wasteful. Many communities erected municipal crematoriums and memorial gardens, making this service available at nominal cost.

Cremation has become so popular that difficulties are reported in scheduling the large number of cremations, particularly on weekends when it is more convenient for families to attend funerals. At times families will postpone cremation for a week or more to have cremation scheduled on a Saturday.

Latest statistics indicate that in 1966 there were 195 crematoriums operating in Great Britain; there were 294,134 cremations, representing 46.9 per cent of the total number of deaths during that year.

The United States

Development of modern interest in cremation in the United States has in many respects been quite similar to that in Europe. Although cremation had been used by various Indian tribes in America, the colonists and their descendants practiced earth burial according to the customs of their homelands. There are two recorded instances of cremations in South Carolina shortly before 1800. These cremations were done with funeral pyres and were arranged at the request of those who were cremated.

A small number of interested people in New York City held a series of meetings in 1873–74 to discuss cremation. However, there was so little public support that plans to establish a crematorium were soon abandoned.

In 1876 a physician in Washington, Pa., Dr. Julius Lemoyne, constructed a crematorium on his own property. He shared the concern for public health that had moved many of his European colleagues. His crematorium was built primarily to dispose of his own body when he died. Because of his desire that people understand the advantages of cremation he permitted several advocates of the practice to make use of the crematorium at the time of their death. Thus in 1876 the first modern cremation in the United States was carried out.

The first crematorium owned and operated by a society was built in Lancaster, Pa., in 1884. Other facilities were established on this basis in major cities, although the development was not rapid. Most of the crematoriums were owned by societies; a few were owned by a municipality, by a fraternal order or by a church. By the turn of the twentieth century there were twenty-six in operation. Bodies were often transported considerable distances by rail to the nearest crematorium.

Local cremation societies were founded with a dual purpose: to operate crematoriums and to educate the public. Several journals were published in the interests of cremation, although they survived for only a few years. The narrow focus of their concerns necessarily dictated that the arguments in favor of cremation be reiterated again and again, and reader interest was very difficult to sustain.

Early supporters of cremation in the United States fall into several categories. Some cremation societies were organized in cities with sizable German populations whose members carried on some of the thought and practice of the liberal rationalists of the mid-nineteenth century. Other groups were organized by liberal Protestant clergymen concerned with reform of funeral practices. Other proponents of cremation were members of the medical profession reacting against the serious health problems associated with earth burial.[25]

These local societies joined in 1913 to form the Cremation Society of America with Hugo Erichsen, M.D.,

---

[25] Cf. Robert W. Habenstein and William M. Lamers, *The History of American Funeral Directing* (Rev. ed; Milwaukee: Bulfin Printers, 1962), p. 455.

as president. His presidential address shows the reforming fervor of the movement at that time:

> Every crematist must be a missionary for the cause, and embrace every suitable occasion to spread its gospel, the glad tidings of a more sanitary and more aesthetic method of disposing of our beloved dead.[26]

A similar international organization was formed as the International Cremation Federation in 1937. This federation is concerned with advancing the use of modern cremation throughout the world.

The Cremation Association of America is the lineal descendant of the society formed by Dr. Erichsen. It has, however, a different format and purpose than the original body. It is an organization of the managements of privately owned crematoriums and columbariums in the United States and Canada.

In the president's address of 1963, the fiftieth anniversary of the founding of the association, Clifford Zell, Jr. stated:

> When one looks back, I cannot help but feel that the early days of the Cremation Association of America are just what that word implies, an interested group of men concerning themselves with the process of preparation with little constructive thought to the important job of helping to dignify the memorials of families' thoughts to the memory of their loved ones departed. . . .
> As we mark our 50th anniversary, we might well give thought to this—would we be so far wrong to call ourselves the Columbarium Association of America? My thinking is certainly upon those lines. As embalming is to the funeral ceremony, as grave digging is to the cemetery service, we might do well

[26] *Ibid.*, p. 457.

> to think of cremation in relation to the niche and urn for these are truly the product we represent.[27]

Cremation is not making the rapid strides in the United States that it is in England. In recent years there have been 600 to 1000 more cremations each year, which is not in proportion to the increasing population. The total number of cremations in the United States in 1964 was 67,658. This is about three to four per cent of the total number of deaths in that year.

THE CHANGING MOTIVATIONS FOR CREMATION

A simple historical survey of cremation practices may be of limited interest, but it is far more significant to trace the very important shifts which have taken place in the reasons for man's practice of cremation. As we shall see in describing these motivational patterns, these changes do not merely represent variations in particular reasons for cremation. Even more noteworthy is the change in the categories or configurations of reasons.

Prehistoric Times

It appears that cremation for prehistoric man was predominantly religiously motivated. Of course, because we are dealing with a prehistoric and preliterate period, we can only speculate about the reasons behind the practice of cremation. Yet, on the basis of archeological findings and speculation founded on cultural anthropological studies of very primitive cultures, some opinions can be ventured.

The simple dualism in even the most primitive forms of animism may well account for some of the motivation for cremation. It may well be that the speedy free-

[27] *Forty-fifth Convention of the Cremation Association of America* (Fresno, Calif.: The Cremation Association of America, 1963), p. 9.

ing by fire of the animating spirit from the decay of the body was behind much of the practice of cremation. The rapid dissolution of the body is a desirable objective for one with dualistic assumptions.

It may well be that the evident reduction in the burning process was interpreted as purifying. Thus cremation would be a means for purifying both body and spirit from the awesome taboos growing out of the fear of death. A corollary of this might be the possible interpretation of cremation as sacrifice. The deification of fire was not unknown, and to consign a dead body to fire may well have had religious significance.

Sometimes a kind of eschatological meaning may have been attached. There is no evidence of a universal or consistent interpretation of this nature, but there are indications that for some people cremation may have represented a belief that after death the spirit went to the sun or rose with the smoke of the pyre to the skies. Dissolution of the body was accomplished in a way representative of the understanding of freeing the spirit and conveying it to its ultimate destination.

Some form of preparation of charred bones made possible continued contact with some portion of the person of the deceased, even though in radically changed form. This may have been associated with some primitive beliefs about the continued existence in the grave. A kind of "tangible permanence" was retained.

Thus it would appear that the possible very early motivations for cremation, as well as for other forms of disposition, were primarily religious. The development of a cult of the dead in prehistoric times makes this quite conceivable. To this we may add the possible secondary motivation of sanitation, growing out of a simple folk wisdom in reaction to the obvious unpleasantness of an unattended dead body.

The Ancient World

In the world of the Greeks and the Romans, the persistence of religious motivation can be noted. It was a means for quickly freeing the spirit from its bodily prison and thus enabling it to leave the community of the living. The ghost was free to go to the spirit world rather than linger about the body. Thus cremation would be particularly effective for disposing of the bodies of those against whom society wanted to defend itself: criminals, outcasts, sorcerers. So in some cultures, such as the Jewish, cremation would be motivated, in its exceptional usage, as a punitive measure.

Far more common in the ancient world was the understanding of the freeing of the spirit by cremation seen in some of the more sophisticated developments of Greek philosophy. The disembodied spirit was totally unencumbered by the strictures of material existence with its uncleanness and finitude. The destruction of the mortal dimension of man left only that which is immortal. Cremation could thus be understood as a part of the religious process of spiritual refinement.

But during this era some practical considerations were added to the religious motivations. There is good reason to believe that cremation first became common among wandering tribal societies. As the cult of the dead developed it was more important to care continually for the remains of the deceased. The mobility of the tribe made it difficult to care for or defend permanent grave sites. To avoid neglecting the graves and to preclude despoiling of the graves by enemies, it was better to cremate and carry the remains of the dead along with the tribe. Where superstition required that survivors protect themselves from reprisals by offended spirits of the dead because of failure to care for the dead properly, cremation was an expedient solution.

In the ancient world we can also see emergence of explicit concerns for sanitation and health. While we cannot be sure how early such concerns appeared, we do know that it was at least as early as the fifth century B.C. The fact that fire was regarded as purifying and reducing would suggest it as a solution to the problem, even in the absence of any knowledge of bacteria and sterilization.

So we see in the ancient world a continuation of the religious motivation, which appears to have been designed to do something to and for the dead, and some practical motivations more intended for the living.

The Nineteenth Century

Following the long eclipse of cremation in the Western world from the fourth century A.D. on, we find a resumption of some of the old patterns, discontinuation of others and the acknowledgment of a number of new reasons for practicing cremation.

The religious motivations for cremation seen in earlier periods do not play much of a part in the modern cremation movement. Although a few liberal clergymen were supporters of the movement, most of the weight of the religious establishment was thrown against the practice. While numerous theological arguments were used by the opponents of cremation, the supporters limited themselves to answering these objections and rarely advanced theological arguments in favor of cremation. There were some humanitarian concerns evident but there was no explicitly religious motivation involved.

Much of the motivating force behind cremation grew out of health concerns. This was not really new, but the advance of scientific medicine began to give it new weight. Bacteriology showed the nature of problems arising from the terrible condition of overcrowded graveyards. Pasteur and Koch showed that disease was often communicated by pollution. Many of the articles supporting cremation were written by physicians who described in detail, often lurid, the way in which air and water pollution from cemeteries caused numerous deaths. An address before the New England Cremation Society in 1891 illustrates the health emphasis:

> The object of placing a dead body beneath, rather than upon, the surface of the ground, is that the earth may absorb and neutralize the products of gradual decomposition. This result is very imperfectly accomplished. The volatile forms escape into the air in the form of noxious gases; and this, it would seem, almost without regard to the depth at which the body may have been interred. Those which cannot thus escape find their way into the springs and watercourses of the vicinity. Thus the inhabitants of the locality are compelled to breathe and drink that which has been contaminated with these poisonous emanations.[28]

These dangers could be avoided by the speedy and safe disposition of the remains through cremation.

Economic motivation was not strongly advanced although it was present. Where once cremation had been so expensive that the poorer people could not utilize it, there were in the modern period occasional references to the fact that the process of cremation was less costly than burial. However, because many of the early cremations in the United States involved transporting the body considerable distances to the nearest crematorium, the process may have been fairly costly when viewed totally. While cremation was economical for some, it was not universally so; hence this motivating force was not prominent.

A considerable number of new reasons for cremation

[28] John S. Cobb, *A Quarter-Century of Cremation in North America* (Boston: Knight & Millet, 1901), pp. 170–71.

emerged during the rebirth of cremation in the nineteenth century. These are seen in numerous articles in *The Modern Crematist,* a journal published in Lancaster, Pa., in the late 1880's.

There was considerable emphasis on aesthetic motivation. Terrifying word pictures were painted of the process of decay. "Cremation commends itself promptly to the good judgment of thoughtful people . . . whose sensibilities recoil from the abominable thought of encoffined rottenness with its nameless horrors."[29] Cremation was a way for avoiding this awful experience by providing almost immediate dissolution of the body. A second part of this pattern was that cremation was a way of avoiding the horror of being buried alive. We know from alarm devices built into caskets and various escape mechanisms patented during this period that this was a cause of considerable concern to many people prior to the days of arterial embalming. Gruesome tales circulated of individuals who were discovered to have been interred while in a deep coma or cataleptic state only to revive after burial. Cremation precluded, although drastically, this unfortunate occurrence. The aesthetic motivation favoring cremation provided certain comforts to the individual by sparing him the unpleasant contemplation of decomposition or of premature burial.

Other very practical new motivations entered the picture at this time. In order to secure cadavers for medical dissection, anatomists sometimes bought bodies which had been disinterred by grave robbers.

> In these days of "body snatching," there is no certainty that the form which we loved, and was once the temple of the Most High God, and which we watched lowered into the grave with Christian

[29] *The Modern Crematist,* I, No. 1 (1886), 1.

rites—there is no certainty that this form rests there in peace.[30]

Cremation commended itself to some as a protection against such body snatching.

Another of these practical appeals involved avoidance of the practice of removal of graves which was sometimes required by urban growth. Many people responded negatively to the idea of disinterment and reburial.

> That which remains of the bodies so carefully and tearfully laid in graves and vaults constructed for their reception is taken out with picks and shovels of rough and hardened laborers as devoid of sentiment as are the tools they handle. Amid profanity and, in many cases, gross obscenity, they are loaded promiscuously into carts and carried off. . . .[31]

Such a problem would not exist if cremation were practiced: this was the line of argument.

One of the major practical reasons for cremation was land usage, particularly in England. This reason was often coupled with that of sanitation. Cremation made extensive cemeteries unnecessary, thus conserving valuable land in urbanizing societies.

Another new reason for cremation was progress. It appealed to those who were liberal in disposition, who were moved by the social change that was sweeping across the Western world, who were seeking to bring new patterns of custom to replace those forms which were aging. At times this almost degenerated to novelty for the sake of novelty as proposals were advanced which departed far from ideas people were accustomed to hold. Erichsen describes a proposal made for producing illuminating gas as a by-product of cremation and an-

[30] Henry H. Bonnell, *Cremation: Scientifically and Religiously Considered* (Philadelphia: Press of D. C. Chalfant, 1885), p. 7.

[31] Cobb, *op. cit.*, p. 179.

other by Sir Henry Thompson who suggested the use of the ashes as a commercial fertilizer.[32] Needless to say, these suggestions did little to advance the cause of cremation but they do serve to show the openness to new ideas which characterized advocates of cremation.

The last reason for cremation advanced during this period was convenience. Since the early crematoriums had chapels as part of the building in many instances, it was pointed out that the entire funeral could be carried out indoors. Thus persons in attendance were not exposed to the elements in inclement weather.

Contemporary Motivational Patterns

One final step must be taken in this listing of motivations for cremation in various periods. We need to examine the status of these various reasons at the present time to see how motivational patterns have changed.

Today, very few discussions of cremation deal with religious motivation for cremation. The contemporary advocates of cremation largely see it as a matter with no religious significance. The separation of body and spirit is not crucial to the thought of man today. Purification of the spirit or the body has no religious significance.

Nor is sanitation a predominant reason for cremation at present. Modern embalming and burial techniques have drastically reduced the dangers to public health that once existed in graveyards.

What we have spoken of as aesthetic motivation, abhorrence of deterioration in the grave, etc., is regarded largely as a matter of personal preference. For some this might be a reason for being cremated but it does not appear to be prevalent.

Land use is an increasing problem in the growth of large metropolitan regions. The sheer inconvenience of

[32] Erichsen, *op. cit.*, pp. 157, 159.

having cemeteries located miles away from one's home has caused some to prefer cremation. In England we see rapid growth of cremation, attributed in sizable measure to difficulty in continuing to provide suitable space for burial in many communities.

Population mobility also appears to contribute to motivation for cremation. The fact that many families move about from place to place frequently has made it difficult to maintain family burial plots in many locations. Some families prefer to cremate at the time of death and return the ashes to the original family home. Whereas transportation of the body would be difficult, the shipment of the ashes is easy and inexpensive. The fact that so many cremations in the United States take place on the West Coast where many families have migrated from other sections of the country has caused some to speculate that mobility is a fairly common motivating factor for cremation.

For some, economic motivations are also part of present-day preference for cremation. This economic motivation has two sides, which appear to be somewhat contradictory. On the one hand, cremation is normally less costly than burial. On the other hand, the profit motive plays a part as cremation interests encourage the practice as a means of fostering memorialization.

Finally, there is the emergence of psychological motivation for cremation, reasons growing out of the psychological understanding of bereavement which point to aspects of the cremation process which are possibly, but not necessarily, helpful. These will be dealt with more fully in a later chapter.

So we conclude the survey of cremation from prehistoric times to the present. We shall return in a number of ways to the contemporary elements of the motivational shifts just described.

Cremation
Today

FUNERARY customs are normally subject to broad local variations. Consequently, any description of the process of cremation will not be universally accurate in all details. An account of the overall structure of the process will, however, be generally applicable.

THE PROCESS OF CREMATION

The actual position of the act of cremation in the patterned activities following death can be any one of four variations. In some instances the customary pattern will be followed up to the time of committal. The preparation of the body, the viewing, the funeral will be held as usual. Then, instead of going to the cemetery for burial, the body and the mourners will go to the crematorium for committal and disposition.

A second variation is to have the funeral service in the crematorium chapel, much as it might be held in a funeral home, followed by committal and cremation.

At times the body may be prepared and then taken to the crematorium for viewing and the funeral. Some

English crematoriums have "chapels of rest" very similar to the rooms found in American funeral homes for the purpose of viewing and visitation of the bereaved family.

A fourth option is to have the body taken to the crematorium by the funeral director as soon as possible after death. It is then cremated privately and a public memorial service may be held later at the convenience of the family.

In all but the fourth pattern a ritual act of committal is normally included. This often takes place in the chapel of the crematorium, even though the funeral may have been held elsewhere. Following the service of committal the casket is removed to the committal chamber according to the practice of the particular crematorium. In some the catafalque is mechanically equipped either to lower the casket through the floor, much as into the grave, or to slide the casket mechanically through a door into the committal chamber. In some other crematoriums a curtain is drawn between the mourners and the catafalque, and the casket is removed. In yet others the casket on a movable catafalque is rolled from the chapel to an adjacent room by the staff either while the people are yet assembled or after they have left the chapel.

The committal chamber, a small room with access to the cremation furnaces, is usually arranged in much the same decor as the chapel. The opening to the furnace is usually a part of a stone or paneled wall. Behind this is the metal door to the cremation chamber which is only of sufficient size to receive the casket. Members of the family or their representative may watch the casket placed in the cremation chamber. Sometimes a witness is designated by the family to be present at the beginning of the process in order that they may be assured that the cremation has actually taken place.

Flowers are not put into the furnace but a few representative blossoms may be laid on the casket. This is to avoid introducing into the furnace the noncombustible wires that are part of so many floral arrangements.

Once the casket is in the cremation chamber intense heat is applied by a series of oil or gas flames. The process normally requires about one and a half hours to complete. Because of the intense heat and the scientific draft control in the specially designed furnaces, combustible gases are recirculated until virtually no smoke is visible. Just as decomposition in the earth is oxidation, so cremation is a process of very rapid oxidation of the body tissues. The water content the body is evaporated by the intense heat, the carbon-containing portions of the body are incinerated and the inorganic ash of the bone structure is all that remains. The residue of the average-sized individual comprises about five to seven pounds of ash and bone fragments.

When the combustion chamber has cooled, the residue is collected. Metallic parts of the casket are withdrawn from the ashes with a magnet. The ashes are then placed in a temporary container or in an urn purchased by the family. In England it is common that the ashes are mechanically pulverized into a fine powder. This is not often done in the United States, although some crematoriums will reduce the larger bone fragments to a pebble-like consistency.

The ashes are then returned to the funeral director or to the authorized member of the family for final disposition. There are a number of options available at this point. The family may purchase an urn and a niche in the columbarium of a crematorium. Or an urn may be purchased for burial in a family plot or in an urn garden especially designed for the interment of ashes. Or the cremated remains may be kept by the family or stored by the crematorium to be disposed of at a later time, such as at the time of the death of the surviving spouse. It is possible in all but a few western states to have the ashes strewn or scattered. This may be done at some later time by the crematorium staff or, if there is no public nuisance created, by the family or their representative at some place of special significance for them.

Occasionally another brief service of committal is held at the time of the final placement of the ashes. The Cremation Association of America strongly recommends that such a service be conducted to dignify the disposition of the ashes as something more than mere discard. The Anglican church also urges that strewing of ashes in "gardens of remembrance" be done under the supervision of a clergyman and that it be done on consecrated ground.

Suitable memorial inscriptions are usually made on the front of the niche where the ashes are placed. In England, where most ashes are scattered in crematorium gardens, there are "books of remembrance" in which the name of the deceased is inscribed, and it is possible to place a small metal plaque, bearing the name of the person, on a memorial wall or in the garden.

THE CREMATORIUM

Most crematoriums are constructed with the following features: a waiting room for mourners, a chapel, a committal chamber, a cremation chamber, an office and urn selection room and a columbarium. Architectural styles vary from Gothic modifications to contemporary forms. In many instances a parklike setting surrounds the crematorium.

MANAGEMENT

Ownership and management patterns vary widely from country to country. In England most of the crematiums are owned and operated by municipal or regional authorities. Efforts are being made to provide crematoriums for even the most rural areas of the country. In the United States there are over 200 crematoriums. The vast majority of these are owned and operated by cemetery managements. Some are owned by corporations operating exclusively as crematoriums and columbariums. Some are owned and operated by funeral directors. A very small number, less than five per cent of the total, are government owned.[1]

In some areas there has been interest on the part of churches in setting up columbariums in their buildings, much as churches once had their own graveyards.

EMPHASIS

The fact that crematoriums in the United States are commercially operated directs to some extent the emphasis found in the enterprise. Crematorium staffs are urged to: "Talk less about cremation, crematory, incineration, and more about columbarium, memorials, chapels, gardens, perpetual care, light, flowers and art."[2] This emphasis is further defined: ". . . we should always realize that cremation is but preparation of the deceased for inurnment or interment. . . . The emphasis should be placed on the completion of the inurnment or interment and not on the preliminary step of cremation."[3]

The municipal management of most English crematoriums brings a somewhat different emphasis. Sir John Cameron, speaking as president of the Cremation Society, said:

[1] Cf. Robert W. Habenstein and William M. Lamers, *The History of American Funeral Directing* (Rev. ed.; Milwaukee: Bulfin Printers, 1962), p. 589.

[2] *Manual of Standard Crematory-Columbarium Practices* (Interment Association of California, 1941), p. 15.

[3] *Ibid.*, p. 5.

Our aim must always be to bring cremation within the scope of the great masses of the people and to provide an economic service which will render the wasteful and extravagant procedure of burial completely unacceptable. Most cremation authorities genuinely seek this ideal, but many are handicapped in doing so by increasing overhead costs, and in particular, costs over which they have no control.[4]

REGULATION

Crematorium and columbarium operators in the United States are subject to two kinds of regulation. One of these is the mandatory obligation to the laws of the state in which the crematorium is operated. The other is the advisory regulation of the *Manual of Standard Crematory-Columbarium Practices* of the Cremation Association of America.

The mandatory legal regulation of cremation has largely to do with the authorization of cremation by the legal custodian of the body of the deceased and by the government officer who certifies the cause of death and issues the necessary permit for cremation. We shall deal with the legal aspects of cremation in more detail in a later chapter.

The Cremation Association of America does not have binding regulations but advises its members according to a consensus on proper operation of crematoriums and columbariums. There are a number of major areas of concern where such advisory regulation is given.

Crematorium managements are urged to secure proper authorization from the next of kin for the cremation of the deceased and for suitable disposition of the ashes. Careful and permanent records of all cremations are to be kept.

There are also suggested regulations regarding the

[4] *Pharos,* XXVI, No. 3 (1960), p. 19.

casket. Although state laws in many instances do not require it, most crematoriums will not cremate unless the body is in a suitable container.

> The rules and regulations of each crematory should provide that all human remains intended for cremation be received at the crematory in a suitable casket, and should not be placed in the cremation chamber without being in an acceptable container. And by acceptable container is meant one which will insure protection to the health and safety of the operator, provide a proper covering for the remains, meet minimum requirements for the maintenance of appropriate respect and consideration and composed of suitable combustible material.[5]

A suitable container can be anything from a very modestly priced pine box to a more costly wooden or metal casket. The Cremation Association of America in its *Manual of Standard Crematory-Columbarium Practices* suggests that casket selection be made in just the same way as it is for earth burial, since in either cremation or interment the casket is ultimately inaccessible for further use.

In the very early days of the modern cremation movement the body was customarily removed from the casket before being placed in the cremation furnace. This is no longer done. If a wooden casket is used, it is completely incinerated, and the few ashes, because of their lightness, tend to pass through the flue. If a metal casket is used, the body is cremated within the casket. After a period of cooling the remains are collected from within the burnt-out casket.

The only effort to regulate the kind of casket used refers to the practical matter of combustibility. Crema-

---

[5] Herbert Hargraves in the proceedings of the *Forty-third Convention, Cremation Association of America* (Cremation Association of America, 1961), p. 82.

toriums regard as unacceptable certain types of plastic or fiberglass caskets which would create excessive smoke in the incineration process or which would melt and fuse with the remains of the body in the cremation chamber.

Proposed regulations for the operators of columbariums are included in the manual.

> One of the predominant arguments used by all columbarium representatives in arranging for space in the building is "permanency." . . . The columbarium that allows anything but a permanent receptacle to go into its niches is being inconsistent.[6]

In part this concern is economically motivated and in part it is an effort to express the sense of obligation of columbarium managers to keep faith with their aim of relatively permanent memorialization.

The ethical responsibilities described for crematorium operation have several facets. There is heavy emphasis upon the respectful handling of the body of the deceased and the cremated remains. Crematorium staffs are instructed to deal with the body of the deceased as they would with those of members of their own families. There is also strong regard for privacy. Visitors are not permitted in the crematorium when cremations are in progress. Only witnesses designated by the family are allowed to be present when the process is begun. The crematorium is also responsible for careful identification of the ashes so that they may be returned to the proper family. Most crematoriums do this by placing a registered numbered metallic disc in the cremation chamber with the casket to provide for subsequent identification of the ashes.

The regulations proposed for crematoriums give special attention to the language and terminology used by their representatives.

[6] *Manual of Standard Crematory-Columbarium Practices,* p. 12.

> . . . your choice of words, both before and after
> cremation, should encourage memorialization of
> remains. Using proper phraseology not only helps
> the bereaved but also creates the desire for a
> memorial.[7]

The proposed terminology includes the defining of cremation as a "preparation for inurnment or interment";
the use of the terms "cremated remains" or "human remains" instead of "ashes," because ashes connote scattering; the removal of the harshness of the word "retort"
and the substitution of "cremation chamber." It is interesting to note that cremation literature in England
commonly uses such terms as "ashes," "cremation
furnace" and "disposal."

RELATIONSHIP WITH FUNERAL DIRECTORS

One of the sensitive points in the practice of cremation in the United States at present involves the relationship between crematoriums and funeral directors.

In a few instances this is no problem at all because
some crematoriums are owned and operated by funeral
service establishments. In this way a few funeral directors offer to their patrons an additional service. This,
however, is by far the exception rather than the rule.

The Cremation Association of America recognizes the
activities of its members as a supplement to the services
of a funeral director. It answers the question: Is a funeral
director necessary? by saying, "His services are exactly
the same as for other forms of care and his services are
needed for the first call, embalming, casket selection
and conduct of the funeral."[8]

Still, most funeral directors tend to be less than en-
thusiastic about cremation. "Those funeral directors who

[7] *Ibid.,* p. 5.
[8] *Cremation: The Way of Nature* (Cremation Association of
America).

operate crematories assert that they are providing another type of service, but for the majority of funeral directors, cremation is held to be a matter of personal choice, and their inclination is neither to encourage nor actively to resist the practice."[9]

Discussions with both funeral directors and crematorium managers reveal a mutual suspicion of conflicting interests. The crematorium management feels that funeral directors, through laws which require a licensed funeral director to secure certification of death and permission to bury or cremate, have made themselves indispensible adjuncts to the cremation process. Furthermore there is the feeling that funeral directors tend to resist cremation because of the connotations of economy or because of the possibility of encouraging simple disposal. Funeral directors, on the other hand, often see in the advocates of cremation, not necessarily identical with crematorium managements, potential reformers of funeral practice, critics of the economics of the funeral and exponents of minimal funeral arrangements. Thus there is a pervasive hesitancy to support actively the practice of cremation, although virtually any funeral director, unless he has personal religious scruples against it or unless he senses that mourners are too overwrought to make decisions responsibly, would co-operate with the request of a bereaved family to have cremation of the body of the deceased.

So we see that, because of state laws requiring the participation of a licensed funeral director, the cremation management is necessarily dependent on co-operation with funeral directors. At the same time, many funeral directors are fearful of the implications of widespread adoption of cremation in the United States and

[9] Habenstein and Lamers, *op. cit.*, p. 589.

the possible reverberations in the economics of funeral practice.

THE DISPOSITION OF THE ASHES

We have noted that one of the significant variations between cremation in England and cremation in the United States has to do with the promotional emphasis. In England, which has a normative quality because of the rapidly increasing acceptance of cremation in a culture similar in most respects to our own, the major emphasis is on the encouragement of public acceptance of cremation as a mode of disposition of the body. There is little specific emphasis on what is done with the ashes following cremation, although this does not mean that there is crude indifference to final disposition.

In the United States, relatively little attention is given to securing public acceptance of the practice through extensive education or promotion. The far greater emphasis is on the way in which the cremated remains are memorialized following cremation. As we have already indicated, cremation is seen merely as preparation for inurnment.

Thus a great deal of attention is given by American crematoriums and columbariums to developing particular patterns for final disposition of the ashes. In both England and the United States the same options exist, but the practices of the two countries have moved along quite different lines since the beginning of the modern cremation movement.

First of all, some families will elect to receive the ashes and to inter them in a family burial plot or in a special cemetery for cremated remains called an urn garden. These ashes can be buried either in an urn purchased for that purpose or in the temporary container in which the crematorium returns the ashes. Each cemetery has its own conditions regulating the interment of cremated remains. Individual or family plots in urn gardens, because of their small size, are naturally somewhat less costly than regular burial lots. A monument can be erected in some instances or a small plaque placed at the site of the burial.

The second option is that of purchasing a niche in a columbarium, very often one which is in connection with the crematorium. Niches to hold one or several urns can be purchased. Prices vary with the location and size of the niche. The ashes are placed in an urn which has been purchased. The niche is then closed with a bronze cover inscribed with the name of the deceased or with a plate glass front which leaves the urn in view. Some columbariums have different rooms in which niches can be purchased. Some of these have niches arranged as shelves and bronze urns in the shape of books placed upon the shelves. Usually a selection of urns ranging in price from approximately fifty dollars to several hundred dollars is available. Niches vary in price but are normally comparable with the price of graves in the given region. Perpetual care arrangements are usually included in the cost of the niches.

A third option is that of strewing or scattering the ashes upon the ground. In England this is an extremely popular method, with the ashes of about ninety per cent of those cremated being strewn. The crematoriums have lovely gardens of remembrance with roses, flowering shrubs and lawns. Because the Anglican church requires that Christians be buried in consecrated ground, portions of gardens of remembrance may be consecrated by the Church of England. Usually the ashes are deposited over a very limited area by a member of the crematorium staff using a special container designed to sprinkle them on the ground rather than broadcast them indiscriminately. The ground is then lightly raked. Usually the family is not present for the strewing, although the Church of England strongly suggests that a clergyman have part in the final disposition. Memorial plaques may be placed in the gardens, or on a wall designed for that purpose. Or the name of the deceased may be inscribed in a large ornate book of remembrance which is on display in the crematorium.

The Cremation Association of America, because of its interest in memorialization, has strongly opposed strewing of the ashes. The Interment Association of California has stated: "The only proper disposition of cremated remains is inurnment in a niche, a vault, or an urn garden or in a recognized place for interment of human dead."[10]

A variety of ways have been followed to discourage the practice of strewing. In several states legislation has been passed prohibiting scattering of cremated remains.

Strong disapproval of the use of the term "ashes" is another way in which strewing is discouraged.

> In using that word we . . . encourage scattering, for what is more natural than to scatter "ashes"? The correct description of the residue of cremation is "cremated remains" or "human remains," because they are not "ashes" but fragments of human bones. With this description there is an encouragement to memorialize rather than to destroy.[11]

The assumption is that strewing is undignified discarding of what is left of the body or subjecting it to possible despoilment. Members of the Cremation Association have available pictures or specimens of cremated remains showing recognizable bone fragments several inches in length. This is intended to show that scattering

[10] *Manual of Standard Interment Practices and Standard Crematory-Columbarium Practices* (Los Angeles: Interment Association of California, 1941), p. 23.

[11] *Manual of Standard Crematory-Columbarium Practices*, p. 5.

is unsuitable because persons would see the portions of calcined bone or animals might carry them off. It is also pointed out that even with the drastic reduction of the body in cremation, there is still something of the person present which should be memorialized. The suggestion of spreading about five to seven pounds of fragments of bones of a loved one is naturally quite distasteful to many.

In England this problem is solved by mechanical pulverization of the ashes into fine powder which is easily and inoffensively mixed with the soil of the garden of remembrance. Electrically operated pulverizers especially designed for this purpose are part of the standard crematorium equipment. This practice is strongly resisted in crematoriums in the United States.

> Never crush or grind cremated remains. . . . They should be placed in the temporary container or urn as they are removed from the cremation vault . . . To do otherwise encourages desecration, gives the impression of valueless ash and will eventually destroy the memorial idea.[12]

Some form of crushing of the fragments is a necessary prelude to the practice of strewing the ashes. It need not be less dignified nor less respectful than committing the body to the grave or to the cremation furnace.

Apart from the economic ramifications for columbariums of these various means of disposing of the ashes there is another consideration. How important is it for mourners to have a specific location for the remains of the dead?

The various means of disposition indicate something of the intentions of the mourners. Some wish to have a place which will stimulate their recollections of the deceased. Some wish to symbolize the unity of life with

[12] *Ibid.*, p. 8.

all of nature by blending the ashes into the natural elements of the earth. Some wish to deposit the remains in a place of particular meaning or sentiment for the deceased and the mourners.

MEMORIALIZATION

Leaving aside the commercial dimensions, whether they be understood as protection for the manufacture and sale of urns and niches, or the pride of possession of mourners who achieve status through their purchases, let us look more closely at the reasons for having some identifiable memorial to the dead. There are usually two aspects involved. First of all, it is natural for a person to want his life, in spite of its brevity, to be remembered. Even without a record of world-shaping accomplishments, man wants some mark as a reminder that he has lived. This is consonant with Freud's statement, "At bottom no one believes in his own death, or to put the same thing in another way, in the unconscious everyone of us is convinced of his own immortality."[13] Some sort of tangible memorial is a way of assuring this kind of remembrance, at least for a generation or two.

Similarly, some kind of memorial is important for mourners as a focus for their memories. Of course, if one assumes, as the primitives often do, that the person of the deceased survives in the memorial itself, this can lead to a morbid relationship to the dead. But if this memorial is understood as a tangible symbol of the person who once lived and was loved, who is now dead and remembered, it may be helpful to effective mourning.

This would suggest that there is a value in having some kind of tangible, localized memorial to provide a focus for remembering the deceased. This may or may

[13] Sigmund Freud, "Thoughts for the Times on War and Death" (1915), in *Collected Papers* (New York: Basic Books, 1959), IV, 305.

not directly involve the remains of the body of the one who has died. For some it may be helpful to be able to think of the deceased by knowing that the radically reduced remains of that person's body are in an identifiable niche in a columbarium. They are able to undertake specific acts of remembrance by visiting the columbarium or by placing a flower at the niche as a symbol of their remembering.

Others may find a small bronze plaque or an inscription in a book of remembrance a sufficient focus. The actual ashes of the body of the deceased need not for them be identifiably localized. To know that the remains of the deceased have been respectfully placed in a given general area is enough.

Occasionally plans are made to have the ashes strewn in a familiar place; in the garden of one's home or at a site with some sentimental meaning to the deceased and the mourners. This should be seriously questioned if it provides an offense to others; or if it is a device for trying to keep the deceased person near, causing morbid relational attachments with the deceased to persist.

W. Lloyd Warner, writing from the perspective of social psychology, discusses the significance of cemeteries in a way that casts some light on our discussion here.

> The fundamental *sacred* problem of the graveyard is to provide suitable symbols to refer to and express man's hope of immortality through the sacred belief and ritual of Christianity, and to reduce his anxiety and fear about death as marking the obliteration of his personality—the end of life for himself and for those he loves. . . . The cemetery is an enduring physical emblem, a substantial and visible symbol of this agreement among men that they will not let each other die. . . .
> The fundamental *secular* problem of the graveyard is to rid the living of the decaying corpse, . . . thereby helping to maintain the satisfying images of

themselves as persistent and immortal beings. Another social function of the graveyard is to provide a firm and fixed social place, ritually consecrated for this purpose, where the disturbed sentiments of human beings about their loved dead can settle and find peace and certainty.[14]

Whether a body or ashes, whether a grave or a niche or a memorial plaque is involved is inconsequential, but Warner's insights do help to understand some of the social and psychological values of a focused point of recollection of the dead.

Ideally, mourners should have a full range of options from which to choose the aids to recollecting the deceased. None is really better than another. In every instance death has occurred and relationship has ended, except for the dimension of memory. The only significant question is which particular aids to the remembering process will be most suited to the needs of a particular individual or family.

Preservation of his body or its ashes is not necessary to preservation of memories of him. Inurnment does not necessarily imply excessive attachment to the remains of the deceased, nor does strewing necessarily indicate the disrespectful getting rid of the person and everything about him as if to eradicate the fact of his having lived.

THE ECONOMICS OF CREMATION

Cremation in the United States is a recognizably commercial operation. It is not, as in England, a public utility, but is avowedly a business. The natural goal for the operation of a crematorium and columbarium is to bring a profitable return from the investment in buildings and equipment. The need for profitable operation has

[14] "The City of the Dead," in *Death and Identity*, ed. Robert L. Fulton (New York: John Wiley & Sons, 1965), p. 365.

caused the Cremation Association of America to seek to develop cremation practices along channels which will assure maximum earnings.

The process of cremation is not itself very costly. Prices for cremation are usually seventy-five to a hundred dollars, with some additional charges for extra services, such as the additional cooling time required for cremating in a metal casket. Because the profit of the crematorium is related to the degree of usage, it is desirable to have as many cremations as possible. Since, compared with interment, this is a new practice, it is advisable to keep the cost as low as possible for profitable operation.

It is easy to see that the major income is not from the crematorium but from the sale of space in the columbarium or urn garden and from the sale of urns. This makes the strong emphasis on memorialization understandable. The Cremation Association of America has repeatedly encouraged its members to concentrate their effort on memorializing the dead rather than on promoting cremation itself. An address delivered by Arthur E. Smith at the thirty-seventh convention of the association is a case in point:

> Let's sell memorialization in the enlightened manner, and cremation only as an accelerated process of nature which prepares for memorialization. This not only will get acceptance of the process, but will, by selling the memorialization, promote the sale of urns, niches and our garden plots as well.[15]

This emphasis is implemented not only by the promotion of inurnment but also by active steps to guide toward this practice. The crematorium demonstrates the need for a permanent container for the cremated remains to complete the memorialization process by returning

[15] *Thirty-Seventh Convention of the Cremation Association of America* (Cremation Association of America, 1955).

the ashes in a nonmetallic container. "All crematories should use cardboard containers for the temporary container given with the cremation. . . . It is in no sense suitable for shipping, burial or placement in a niche memorial."[16] Unless the ashes are to be strewn, an urn is thus usually required.

Another way in which the emphasis on memorialization by inurnment is implemented is through the resistance to strewing demonstrated by the Cremation Association as described earlier in this chapter. Its members have secured passage of antiscattering laws in three states and sometimes literature of the industry may imply that this legal prohibition is more widespread.

Many crematoriums would not be unwilling to strew the remains if so requested, although they would prefer not to do so and would seek to discourage the practice. It would be done only by written authorization from the legal custodian of the body of the deceased. Crematoriums will often hold the ashes for several months before strewing because experience has shown them that some families later change their plans. Once the ashes have been scattered, the process is, of course, irreversible. In England the strewing in a garden of remembrance usually takes place within a day or two of the cremation.

Resistance to strewing is in part motivated by fear of what is known as the disposal type of cremation. W. T. Roberts reported that in a survey he made of 1900 cremations on the West Coast there was an increase of disposal type cremations from three per cent to eleven and a half per cent in the years 1961–64.[17]

The disposal type of cremation usually involves cremation immediately following death, with little or no

[16] *Manual of Standard Crematory-Columbarium Practices,* p. 9.
[17] *Forty-seventh Convention of the Cremation Association of America* (Cremation Association of America, 1965), p. 102.

formal memorial service following. The primary aim appears to be to get rid of the body of the deceased as quickly as possible and to attempt to minimize the process of structured mourning. There is no need to go into detail here regarding the possible motivation for such a desire, whether it be a wish to make the process more economical, or to seek to escape from the painful reality of death, or to express the conviction that death so completely destroys the value of the person that any further consideration of value after death is superfluous. It must be realized, however, that disposal is not necessarily synonymous with a wish for simplicity or economy. Memorialization is properly understood to be an attitude rather than a necessary pattern of action.

Naturally, those who would be adversely affected economically by the disposal type of cremation would oppose it. But, as we shall see in a subsequent chapter, there are other vital reasons for questioning the helpfulness of mere disposal in meeting the crisis of bereavement.

The impression should not be given that cremation operators are totally negative in their efforts to guide funerary patterns. As Herbert Philpott expressed it:

> While I do not care to defend this practice [strewing], yet at the same time I do not think that we should be blind to the simple facts that a small percentage of the public insists on having the right to scatter. How long do you think it will be before the cemeteries on this continent offer the English method of working cremated remains into the soil of a rose garden? To resist by the passing of laws is a very doubtful procedure. Public opinion can place the proponents in an uncomfortable and probably untenable position. The public does not look favorably on legislation that establishes fixed methods of displaying sentiment—this is a personal matter.
> The best way to counter the growth of this

practice is to offer a very complete price range of attractive, dignified facilities for proper memorialization.[18]

The fact that the majority of crematoriums in the United States are operated by cemetery managements indicates an existing policy of providing a range of service of either interment or cremation. It is not out of keeping with such a broad policy to provide also a full range of possibilities for disposition of the ashes.

Finally, it should be indicated that, with the commercial basis of crematorium operation in the United States, at the present time the costs connected with cremation and memorialization may be somewhat less than those of earth burial in all of its aspects. To cite specific prices would be difficult because they vary from region to region and because what might appear extravagantly expensive to one family would be regarded as reasonable by another.

As in every aspect of funeral practice, the economic criterion can be applied with legitimacy only when there is careful weighing of the costs against the distinct values received by each family according to its own needs.

[18] *Ibid.*, p. 72.

III

A Psychological
Understanding of
Cremation

JUST as the deepest feelings of individuals and families determine their response to life, so too do they influence their reaction to death and all that accompanies it. This is true not merely of the actual activities involved at the time of death—mourning customs, funeral, burial or cremation—but also of the formation of preferences and plans in advance of the time of death.

As has already been pointed out, various kinds of motivating factors can be traced in the evolving use of cremation. In this chapter, however, we shall be concerned only with discussing motivations discernible in present practice. It is our intention to inquire into both the psychological basis for the selection of cremation as a mode of disposition and the psychological effects of cremation on the mourners.

As we discuss motives for cremation, a distinction must be kept in mind. Some of these motives will be applicable to cremation in general, while others will have to do with the specific uses of cremation immediately following death.

While it is true that every motivation grows in part as a response to an external situation, it is equally true that motives are shaped by the feelings and the inner needs of the individual. Some of these are conscious and rational; others are operating at an unconscious and subrational level. We must seek to explore both dimensions.

CONSCIOUS MOTIVATING FACTORS

Economy

The most easily understood motives for utilizing cremation are convenience and economy. Cremation commends itself in many situations as a practical means to prepare the body for shipping to a distant locality. In a day when well over half of the total population moves during each decade, people become separated by many miles from hometowns and family burial plots. There is still a desire on the part of many families to maintain some sense of rootage, particularly when death unstabilizes life. Thus when death occurs in a family now living in California but with roots in Indiana, there is often the wish to take the body of the deceased back to the place of earlier residence. Cremation offers a distinct advantage at this point. Transportation of a casket and body by rail or air is an expensive operation compared to the shipment of a small box or urn with the ashes of the deceased.

Other economies may be achieved through cremation. The cost is usually reduced because a burial vault is not purchased and because cemetery costs for burying the ashes are less than the cost of opening a grave. Sometimes, however, these economies are offset somewhat by the actual cost of cremation and by the purchase of an expensive urn for the ashes or of premium space in a columbarium.

For those who practice immediate cremation, additional economy is accomplished because embalming is not usually necessary and because a casket of minimum price can be used, since usually the only requirement of the crematorium is that the body be enclosed in a suitable container.

Personal Conviction

Beyond this conscious motivation for cremation founded on very practical considerations there are also individuals and families who are moved by personal conviction to express their preference for cremation. This takes a number of possible forms.

Some express through cremation a modern form of the old dualistic philosophy. Dividing man into material and spiritual components, they seek to enhance the spiritual side of his nature by seeing relatively little value in his physical aspects. Cremation represents for them a way of quickly doing away with the body so that all attention may be devoted to the spirit. This is quite like the ancient understanding of the purification and emancipation of the spirit by the funeral fire. Cremation becomes a means by which the conviction can be expressed that the body is of little importance once the spirit has been separated from it by death.

Another form of conviction sometimes expressed by other advocates of cremation is almost a direct contradiction of the above. Through cremation they express their adherence to a naturalistic monism. All nature is regarded as a unity. Man, then, is totally a part of the natural order in life and in death. When his body ceases to function as a living entity, it is entirely appropriate that it be reduced to its basic elements in the natural world. This end can be accomplished either by cremation or by burial, but cremation affords a particularly effective symbol of quick and direct reduction.

Still another kind of testimony expressed by those who plan cremation may be to their conviction that cremation is aesthetically superior to burial. At one time there was strong sanitarian sentiment expressed in this way, although at present this would rarely be an issue. More likely in our time would be preference for cremation on aesthetic grounds, preferring the speedy dissolution of the body to the slower process of natural decomposition. Or some may dread the notion of being placed in the grave.

Another variation of this conviction would be the expression of disapproval of existing burial or funeral practices by employing cremation. It is not unusual to find cremation strongly supported by groups advocating major reforms in funeral practices. This has been characteristic of numerous phases of the modern cremation movement since its inception. There are a number of reasons for preference on this basis, but one of them seems to be a desire to dramatize the need to rethink old patterns by innovating easily recognizable departures from customary practice. To illustrate, it is not uncommon that immediate cremation has been a medium for seeking to minimize the value or importance of the funeral.

Quite often one finds that the convictions which motivate the selection of cremation are expressed by a number of individuals in the same family. As a result of discussion, a family thus comes to adopt cremation as a part of its practice in meeting the crisis of death because cremation expresses meanings and viewpoints that the family wishes to communicate.

Simplicity

Another of the major factors often constituting a conscious motivation for cremating is a desire for simplicity. As *A Manual for Simple Burial* puts it:

> If some of us at time of death wish to have the
> remains of our loved ones taken promptly and
> quietly for simple burial, or for cremation without
> casket, embalming or ceremony, it is not because we
> are stingy or because we are lacking in sentiment.[1]

Sometimes this represents a desire to simplify the ritual element in funerary customs. The general tendency is toward the elaboration of ritual, even in a culture that is nominally nonritualistic. Ritual is often a way of responding to that which is awesome, mysterious and threatening. The fact that death, for primitive and sophisticate alike, is a traumatic experience, calls for some accustomed ritualistic response. One of the functions of ritual is to enable persons to confront a difficult situation within a structure of responses that have grown from the trial and error of the group. Thus each individual does not have to make a fresh beginning in confronting the crisis. Another function of ritual is an endeavor to communicate in some fairly regularized way the meaning which the group has found valuable in meeting and understanding the crisis. Because of these intended functions, new ways evolve and are added to established customs. Thus ritual becomes elaborated more and more, conserving the things which have been done in the past and adding new elements.

Occasionally there is reaction to this proliferation which takes the form of pruning or cutting back the elaborations. Sometimes the superstructure of ritual has become so unwieldy or has been regarded as so much a thing in itself that it has lost contact with the meanings it was originally intended to convey. Or over periods of time meanings may change, and forms should be altered to adapt to these changed meanings.

[1] *A Manual for Simple Burial* (Burnsville, N. C.: The Celo Press, 1964), p. 13.

This has been the reaction of many funeral reform and memorial society groups. They have felt that intensive reformation is necessary to simplify the practices that have grown up and elaborated around death. One of the avenues for this simplication is cremation, particularly immediate cremation. It reduces the amount of preparation of the body, it does not necessarily involve a funeral or committal service, it can be carried through with no public ceremony.

The trend toward making funerary customs more private is often a part of the process of simplification. There are advocates of cremation who feel that it offers a practical solution. The body is cremated immediately with no public, or even necessarily family, participation. Then, if desired, some ritualized memorial service can be held later.

It is readily apparent that cremation involves no necessary or inevitable simplification. It would be quite possible to include cremation in a very elaborate and expensive funeral. It also would be quite possible to have immediate private burial with minimum preparation and expense, followed by a memorial service. This suggests that there is nothing about cremation itself that automatically produces simplicity or economy. It further suggests that the support for use of cremation may grow out of its variance from the customary pattern. As something different from prevailing custom, it typifies both the discontent with present practice and the proposal of something new, supporting the hope that numerous changes can and shall be made in funerary customs.

Nonconformity

This brings us to yet another of the conscious motivating factors in the selection and practice of cremation: nonconformity. This term is used here descriptively and without judgment. In many communities those who use cremation are those who do not feel particularly bound to established patterns.

American funerary practices are usually rather well established at the community level. Local variations are fairly common, but within a given geographical area, or ethnic group, or religious group, patterns tend to be stable. To deviate from such patterns requires a personal and social security. Security is particularly important in a time of confusion and trauma. This is the reason that bereaved persons so often will accept uncritically patterns with which they do not agree. This tendency to yield to established patterns is due to a number of factors. To accede requires less effort than to resist, and the bereaved often do not have sufficient emotional or physical stamina to swim against the current in a time of crisis. Since conformity is regulated by group pressure, following custom runs less risk of causing offense to others. Because the bereaved require so much the support of others in their time of mourning, they are often particularly sensitive about things that threaten to diminish the support of relatives and friends.

This is not to suggest that those who express their preference for cremation as an exception to community practice are nonconformists just seeking to be different. Rather, in many instances they are expressing their willingness to be different and their security within the social structure.

It is probably no accident that a number of crematorium managers in the United States indicate that many of their clients are well-educated, well-to-do families. These would be the persons who have sufficient community status not to have their security endangered by nonconformity. They are willing to deviate from the customary in order to do what they regard as best.

Avoidance

The last conscious motivation for cremation we would deal with is avoidance. This motivation can be either conscious or unconscious, but it is the former dimension that concerns us here.

The time when cremation is performed is quite important in this regard. Avoidance is related particularly to the practice of immediate cremation. Again, we find this pattern spelled out:

> A simple procedure, whereby the body is removed promptly and with dignity for immediate cremation or burial, after which one or more memorial gatherings are held, can minimize the negative aspects of death and emphasize the deeper meanings and positive values of the occasion.[2]

It is a natural reaction to tend to avoid that which is painful. Thus some bereaved individuals seek to evade those elements of funerary practice that they fear will cause them pain. Quite consciously and deliberately they seek to reduce the number of contacts with other persons, or to shorten the time involved in carrying out a minimum of the established customs, or to remove the body as quickly as possible from sight and interaction so that it is not a focus for any activity of the bereaved.

Immediate cremation is an effective means for achieving these ends. It is very often a private observance; it may involve no family participation at all. It immediately prevents any further contact with the body of the deceased and the pain that this often entails.

It must, however, be pointed out that the mature person recognizes that at times pain is an inevitable part of the healing process. In bereavement the painful awareness that death has taken place, reinforced by seeing the body of the deceased; the painful process of

[2] *Ibid.*, p. 3.

learning to live with memories of the one who has died, and that of sharing with others the deep feelings associated with the loss are elements that contribute to healing. Cremation will be helpful only when it does not obviate or avoid such painful, yet therapeutic, functions.

UNCONSCIOUS MOTIVATING FACTORS

The possible unconscious motivation leading to selection and practice of cremation is much more difficult to describe. It is, of course, much less available to investigation than is the conscious dimension. It is much more highly individual as well.

It is not a new insight that funeral plans sometimes have a hidden agenda. For example, situations are known in which very costly funerals have been purchased to assuage feelings of guilt in the bereaved. Eulogies and accolades sometimes have been planned to compensate for deficiencies in the deceased.

It is possible that cremation, like any other funerary practice, can be used or misused to meet unconscious needs within the bereaved. It should be readily apparent that this involves nothing inherent in cremation itself but describes only the way in which this practice is employed in each instance.

Evasion

Just as we commented earlier on the conscious desire to avoid confrontation with the painful, so too there can be an unconscious variation of the same thing. Even though one has recognized intellectually that confronting reality is necessary to mature development, it is possible that susceptibility to fear of pain would be so great that unconsciously patterns of avoidance would be followed. Or it is possible that a person would seek to evade emotionally stimulating funerary customs because of the belief that a display of feelings would cause others to think less of the mourner. So efforts may be made to plan activities surrounding death to preclude as much as possible any open emotional reaction, to remove as many emotional stimuli as possible, to insulate oneself as fully as possible from reminders of the drastic changes which death has produced. As we have already indicated, cremation, especially immediately following death, can be a means to these ends.

The conscious reasons advanced for cremation may be quite acceptable—simplification, economy—but the commanding unconscious motivation may well be the desire to evade the painful realities of the situation, even though it can be demonstrated that confrontation of that reality is necessary for good mental health.

Control

Another subtle kind of unconscious avoidance pattern is seen in the effort made to create the illusion of controlling death. The way in which contemporary American culture tries to minimize, evade or control death has been described in various places.[3] This is done through the massive attempts to hinder or deny the aging process, the assumption that the medical capacity to postpone death prevents it, or the facade that is built around death. Our way of life and thought is thoroughly permeated by such endeavors.

One response to this need to avoid the reality of death is to seek to gain control over it. In a way the effort to attain a long-term preservation of the body of the dead, from the time of the ancient Egyptians to the present, is a way of trying to assert that as long as the semblance of life is maintained, death is under some

[3] Cf. Paul E. Irion, *The Funeral: Vestige or Value?* (Nashville: Abingdon Press, 1966), pp. 20–43.

measure of human control. It is as if the assumption were that the personality of the deceased persists as long as the physical entity of the body remains reasonably intact.

It is possible that in cremation the unconscious need to control death could make itself felt in exactly the converse way. The fact of man's control is the crucial element in the effort to lessen the threat of death as reality. Just as long-term preservation of the body can be a neurotic attempt at control, so can deliberate dissolution of the body, such as in cremation. Rather than the natural process of decomposition, cremation is man-induced and man-controlled deterioration. Thus, in response to a strong unconscious need to feel in control of death, it could commend itself as an agency for regulating death by controlling the dissolution of the body.

Negative Feelings

Still other unconscious factors are possible components of the decision to cremate. We recognize that strong negative feelings growing out of relationships with the deceased may exist in the bereaved. Although many combinations of such feelings are possible, we shall examine only one: the combination of hostility and guilt.

To illustrate: Sue White was a young married woman who had had through the years a very difficult relationship with her widowed mother. Throughout Sue's adolescence and college years the mother had sought to dominate her existence totally. Sue had passively accepted this domination until her junior year in college when she had met Bill. After a whirlwind courtship, Sue and Bill had been married without her mother's knowledge or consent. The decade that followed was one in which the mother's only overtures of goodwill were thinly veiled attempts to dominate the home of her daughter. Infrequent contacts usually ended in outbursts of anger and frustration.

When Sue's mother died after a long illness, the responsibility for funeral arrangements fell on Sue and Bill as the only close relatives. Sue's mother had expressed no wishes, so decisions were made fully by the young couple. They decided that they would have the body cremated, followed by a memorial service in the home church of the mother.

Sue, as might be expected, experienced a great deal of difficulty in adjusting to the death of her mother. She became quite withdrawn from her normal social contacts and activities. Her husband, her friends, her pastor became concerned for her.

After several weeks of long conversations with her pastor, Sue finally was able to release a good deal of her strong negative feeling, blurting out: "I feel so guilty because I'm just not sorry that my mother is dead. She made life miserable for me for twenty years and I can't shed an honest tear for her!" Then Sue began to talk through a great reservoir of past feelings of hostility and bitterness against her mother from adolescence to the present. She discussed her mother's death and the responsibility for funeral arrangements. She asked: "Do you think that we had my mother's body cremated because we really wanted the break with her to be total and right now?"

The thought that Sue's question suggests is that it is possible to utilize cremation as an aggressive act, even somewhat of a modification of the hostile death wish. Thus intentional destruction of the body could be a form of unconscious wishful destruction of the person.

It is understandable that guilt would very often be present in such cases. If there is the awareness that the presence of the body of the deceased would be a painful reminder of negative relationship, one's guilt may be intensified if that presence is prevented or removed by one's deliberate decision.

This is certainly not to say that cremation produces guilt or that it should produce guilt. Rather we see that where strong hostility toward the deceased and the attendant guilt are felt, these emotions may well be intensified by cremation because it can be understood as a deliberate act of destruction of the body.

This discussion of the extended possibilities for conscious and unconscious motivations lying behind the selection and practice of cremation should indicate that the reasons behind the structuring of funerary practices are really much more important than the question of which practices are chosen. It is possible to use constructively or to misuse many current practices. Which is the case depends largely on our judgment of whether or not a helpful and therapeutic purpose is served by the selection and the practice.

There can be positive, constructive uses of earth burial in which it is recognized by the bereaved that interment represents tangibly and realistically their separation from the body of their loved one, that it marks the termination of that dimension of their relationship centered around the physical presence of the deceased and that the burial is the conclusion of the care which they have exercised toward the one who died.

Whatever form of disposition of the body is used, it should help the mourners to a more profound awareness that death has taken place, that this reality must be accepted, that they can be helped by accepting the pain of mourning and that their relationships with the deceased as they have been known have now ended.

This brings us to the second major part of our consideration of psychological effects of cremation.

PSYCHOLOGICAL EFFECTS OF CREMATION ON THE BEREAVED

Psychologically, cremation can be either advantageous or disadvantageous for the bereaved depending on the way it is understood and the reasons behind the practice.

Advantages

The first major advantage is the way in which cremation can be an aid in accepting reality in the situation of bereavement. When death occurs, it normally is so disruptive to the meaningful relationships of life that it stirs a pervasive sense of unreality. The stable meanings, purposes and values of life are thrown into confusion. Very often the mourner will have the feeling of walking through a bad dream.

If the mourning process is to accomplish its healing function, the bereaved person must face the reality of his situation of loss, even with all its painfulness. Only when he realizes the extent of his loss will he be prepared to begin taking the steps necessary for the reorientation of his life without the presence of the one who has died. To be helped the mourner first has to accept intellectually and emotionally the fact that death has occurred and that it requires of him a major adjustment in his way of living.

Cremation can be a means for reinforcing this acceptance of reality. Properly viewed, its use as a means of disposition is evidence of the fact that death has really occurred and that the person who has died is no longer accessible for relationships as they have been known. The separation of the living and the dead is an important factor in the reinforcement of reality. Morbid grief reactions often involve some attempt to disguise reality or to warp it with illusion. People deceive themselves into feeling that the change is not as drastic as it appears or they hide from their consciousness the fact that the deceased is really separated from them. Death is conceptualized as merely a transition to another slightly different existence. Its effects are minimized as the bereaved tries to maintain illusions that life has not radically changed.

The swift, tangible change in the body of the deceased accomplished by cremation can provide considerable support to the reality of the situation. Furthermore, the ending of life has concluded the usefulness of the body and its speedy reduction into its basic elements reinforces the realistic understanding of man as a part of the natural order. His dying is a part of his living. Dying is a participation in the natural process, just as living is, in spite of the effort of man to seek to minimize its tragic dimensions by thinking of it as unnatural. There is a certain amount of comfort in the knowledge that one's suffering is related to a completely natural process rather than to the arbitrary workings of a malevolent fate.

Closely related to the reinforcement of reality is a second psychological advantage of cremation. It is valuable in providing the bereaved with a sense of finality. An important factor in therapeutic mourning is the realization that life has really ended and that the relationship with the deceased as it has been known has terminated. There are some who confound the mourning process by vain attempts to continue their relationship with the deceased. Sometimes this takes very bizarre forms, such as continuing to set a place at the table for the deceased. More commonly this effort to hold on to the deceased is carried on by assuming that something of the person is still present. Very often this residual element is conceived in terms of the body of the deceased. This is the motivation in many cases for the attempts at long-term preservation of the body. Such efforts to maintain relationships as they have been known are hindrances to the acceptance of reality and impede the necessary activity of seeking to reorient life around living relationships.

Cremation conveys finality by radically changing the composition of the body of the deceased, effectively making it apparent that as the person has been changed, so relational patterns must also change. The person can now only be remembered as he was, and there is no illusion that his bodily presence, even in the grave, is in any sense a basis for relationship.

This finality is best conveyed as the climax of the ritual observances surrounding death. Disposition of the body becomes the last act of the relationship and a logical conclusion to the formal pattern of separation. The ashes, placed in a columbarium or buried, can still provide a focus for remembrance without the morbidity of attempts to maintain a relationship which in reality can no longer exist.

Disadvantages

The psychological disadvantages of cremation are mainly related to the practice of cremation immediately following death. This mode of disposition can be, as we have pointed out earlier, a means of avoidance, thus reducing the value of cremation as a reality-reinforcing mechanism. Immediate cremation also is usually done privately rather than as a part of a public ceremony. This can be a disadvantage because it may prevent therapeutic mourning by isolating the mourner from the group support which is so helpful to him in his bereavement. This will be discussed in detail later.

Again it is necessary to point out that cremation in itself is psychologically neutral. As an aid in adjusting to the traumatic experience of loss through death and the necessary reorientation of life in the process of mourning, its value is determined by the attitudes of the bereaved and the use which they make of it. If it is used for evasion and avoidance of the difficult experiences of dealing with the body of the deceased, or if it is part of an effort to obviate supportive group participation in bereavement, it is not helpful for the readjustment of the mourner to life.

If, on the other hand, it is used to strengthen the realistic acceptance of the occurrence of death and to symbolize the actual conclusion of relationship with the deceased as it has been known, it can be a valuable aid in the therapeutic process of mourning.

IV

Theological Considerations In Cremation

IN early times it is quite probable that cremation had religious significance. In some Eastern religions, such as Hinduism, this is still the case. In Western culture, as we have seen, since the beginning of the Christian era there has been resistance to cremation. As the Christian church extended its influence over Europe, cremation became a virtually extinct practice.

With the rise of the modern cremation movement in the second half of the nineteenth century considerable reaction was evoked in all major Western faiths. Theological objections were raised which became major impediments to the widespread popular acceptance of the practice.

At the present time the issue is being rethought and some modifications are being made in some of the positions formerly held. We shall consider the past and present positions of the Roman Catholic church, of the Protestant churches and of the several branches of Judaism to see the basis for their objections to cremation and the contemporary rationales supporting modifications now being made.

THE ROMAN CATHOLIC POSITION ON CREMATION

The Roman Catholic church in its position against cremation has followed closely the stance of the early Christian church.

The church in the first several centuries of the Christian era, as we have seen, strongly resisted the existing practice of cremation found in much of Europe. Partly this was reaction against practices widely followed by non-Christians. There was also impetus furnished for the early Christian preference for burial over cremation because of a desire to adhere to the customs followed in the burial of the Master. There was also popular sentiment against cremation because it posed questions regarding the resurrection of the body, a germinal part of the Christian hope.

The Roman Catholic church tradition and rule consistently favored burial. As mentioned in an earlier chapter, in 1300 Pope Boniface VIII supported burial as normative practice and threatened with excommunication any who engaged in processes of disposition which circumvented natural deterioration. Those prohibited practices had in part grown out of efforts to prepare bodies for shipment to distant homes from the Crusades.

During this period there was also a growing interest in relics of bodies of the saints. It has been suggested that this interest again supported burial as the normative means for disposing of the dead.

> The superstition which sprang up relating to the miraculous value of the bodies and bones of the dead saints enhanced the value of skeletons. . . . The stamp of priestly authority was given to earth burial, and the bones and bodies of the dead became associated with the religious beliefs of the age.[1]

The Roman Catholic church's position was rarely

[1] *The Modern Crematist*, IV, No. 4 (1889), 50.

enunciated officially until the rise of the modern cremation movement in the late nineteenth century.

When cremations began in Italy in the mid-1880's, the first response of the Roman Catholic church was apparently co-operative. Erichsen reported in 1887 that Roman Catholic priests had not actively opposed the practice of cremation and had, in fact, in Lombardy gone with the body to the crematorium for final prayers.

However, Erichsen's report probably described only the very earliest response because, even before his work was published, official opposition of the Roman Catholic church was being formulated in a statement issued in 1884 by the Congregation of Propaganda.

> No edict was issued by the Councils of the early church against the burning of the dead. It was not until 1884 that the Congregation of Propaganda issued a tentative opinion on the subject recommending passive disapproval—*cremationem approbare non debis, sed passive habeas.*[2]

This passive disapproval, which had been the unofficial position of the Roman Catholic church for some time in spite of the fact that cremation was being practiced in Italy and France, became official in 1886 with the issuance of a series of edicts by Pope Leo XIII. Roman Catholics were forbidden to join cremation societies, to request that their own bodies or the body of someone else be cremated. Roman Catholics who violated these decrees were to be denied burial by the church. In 1892 these decrees were strengthened by excluding violators from receiving the last sacraments.[3]

---

[2] Arnold Wilson and Hermann Levy, *Burial Reform and Funeral Costs* (London: Oxford University Press, 1938), p. 186.

[3] Cf. "Cremation," *The Catholic Encyclopedia,* IV (1908), 482; and Donald W. H. Dorsett, "The Roman Catholic Attitude to Cremation," *Pharos,* XXVIII, No. 3 (1962), 23.

Roman Catholic canon law spells out the resistance of the church to cremation in a number of regulations in the *Corpus Juris Canonici:*

Canon 1203 states:
1. The bodies of the faithful must be buried; their cremation is forbidden.
2. If a person expresses a desire for cremation, it is forbidden to carry out his wish; if the desire is expressed in a testament or otherwise, it shall not be regarded as binding.

Canon 1240 states:
1. Anyone who has requested that his body shall be cremated shall be deprived of ecclesiastical burial unless he has shown signs of repentance before death.
2. If there is any doubt in a case such as above, and time permits, the bishop should be consulted. If there is still any doubt, ecclesiastical burial should be accorded in order to prevent scandal.

Canon 1241 states:
Anyone who has been deprived of ecclesiastical burial will be deprived also of a requiem mass on the anniversary of his death and of all other funeral offices.

Canon 2339 states:
Anyone who seeks to obtain ecclesiastical burial for infidels, apostates, heretics, schismatics or proscripts in accordance with 1241 exposes himself to excommunication of the lower degree (which may be absolved by a priest). If, however, he accords ecclesiastic burial to such he will be subject to a prohibition to enter a church, a punishment which may be suspended only by a bishop.[4]

Such has been the development of the official position

[4] "Cremation and the Canon Law," *Pharos,* XXVII, No. 1 (1961), 3.

of the Roman Catholic church up until recent times. It will be helpful to seek to understand the reasons behind this forceful negative response to the modern cremation movement.

A part of this reaction grows out of consistency with the long tradition of the Christian church in resisting cremation. Burial in consecrated ground has been normative procedure for many centuries for reasons already described. It is important to note that the official opposition of the Roman Catholic church was not based on theological grounds, for cremation has never been held to be in conflict with the dogma of that church.

When one examines the nineteenth century position of the Roman Catholic church, just as in the case of the very early church, one sees that opposition of the church to cremation was largely a matter related to church discipline. Just as the early church resisted cremation as a pagan practice, the Roman Catholic church in the nineteenth century opposed it because of the unorthodox beliefs of some of its protagonists.

Father Dorsett[5] states that the modern cremation movement had its beginning under the French Directory during the fifth year of the republic. He interprets it as allied with the anti-ecclesiasticism of the French Revolution and sees cremation as an attack upon the Christian belief in the immortality of the soul and the resurrection of the body.

The development of cremation in Italy from 1876 onward also had overtones of anticlericalism and anti-ecclesiasticism. The Roman Catholic church, in spite of the fact that the most frequently stated purposes of the advocates of cremation were land usage and public health, saw a threat in that many leaders of cremation

[5] *Op. cit.,* p. 23.

societies were freemasons or agnostics. The 1908 edition of *The Catholic Encyclopedia* shows this.

> The legislation of the Church in forbidding crema-
> tion rests on strong motives; for cremation in the
> majority of cases today is knit up with circumstances
> that make of it a public profession of irreligion and
> materialism. . . . The Church has opposed from the
> beginning a practice which has been used chiefly
> by the enemies of the Christian faith.[6]

It was assumed that cremation was a means of sub-
verting the faithful. Because the church controlled burial
grounds in such predominantly Roman Catholic countries as Italy and France, cremation did provide a
means for evading this control. It is reported that

> The Freemason, Ghisleri, in his *Almanacco dei
> liberi muratori* writes: "Catholics have good reason
> to oppose cremation. The purification of death by fire
> will shake to its foundations Catholic predominance
> based on the terror with which it has surrounded
> death."[7]

That this was a major reason for the opposition of the
Roman Catholic church is further shown by an issue
raised in 1892 by the Archbishop of Freiburg as to
whether a faithful member of the church could co-
operate with the process of cremation as, for example, a
doctor or a municipal official or a laborer in a cemetery.
Judgment was that so long as the person himself did
not agree with the rightness of the process, he could
co-operate if "that cremation is not looked upon as a
distinctive mark of a Masonic sect, that there be nothing
in it which . . . expresses reprobation of Catholic doctrine;
it be not clear that the officials . . . have been assigned
or invited to take part in contempt of the Catholic re-

[6] *Loc. cit.*
[7] Dorsett, *loc. cit.*

ligion."[8] Even as late as 1937 *The Catholic Herald* attributed the church laws against cremation to reaction to those who proclaim disbelief in human immortality and resurrection.[9]

This brings us to yet other reasons for Roman Catholic resistance to cremation. The church regards the process much the same as Tertullian does, as demeaning the dignity of the human body. Cremation is assumed to be dishonoring.

> Reasons based on the spirit of charity and the plain interests of humanity have but strengthened her [the Roman Catholic church] in her opposition. She holds it unseemly that the human body, once the living temple of God, the instrument of heavenly virtue, sanctified so often by the sacraments, should finally be subjected to a treatment that filial piety, conjugal and fraternal love, or even mere friendship seems to revolt against as inhuman.[10]

The reason for this value judgment that cremation is cruel, barbarous, inhuman, dishonoring to the body is not clearly defined. Although there are statements that cremation is contrary only to the laws of the church and not to dogma or divine law, there are occasional inferences in Roman Catholic writers dealing with cremation that the practice is not in keeping with the natural law. For example, the statement that "Cremation also seems opposed to the sentiments of the thoughtful person who believes man was made in the image of God. . . . Cremation may almost be said to encroach on the rights of the Creator and anticipate the work of destruction which belongs to Him alone."[11] It should be pointed

---

[8] *The Catholic Encyclopedia, loc. cit.*
[9] Wilson and Levy, *op. cit.*, p. 187.
[10] *The Catholic Encyclopedia, loc. cit.*
[11] Dorsett, *op. cit.*, p. 21.

out that this view does not appear in the official pronouncements of the Roman Catholic church.

One of the most persistent unofficial reasons for Roman Catholic opposition to cremation is tied to the hope for the resurrection. It is sometimes assumed that dissolution of the body by fire may be a denial of hope for the resurrection.

> There can be little doubt that the practice of cremation in modern Europe was at first stopped, and has since been prevented in great measure, by the Christian doctrine of the resurrection of the body. . . . The objection of the clergy was disposed of by the philanthropist Lord Shaftesbury when he asked, "What would in such a case become of the blessed martyrs?"[12]

We have here a parallel to the situation seen in the early church. There is ample demonstration in the writings of Minucius Felix, Tertullian and Eusebius that Christians were on the defensive against what they understood as attacks on their belief in the resurrection of the body, even though the church itself did not hold that burning prevented resurrection. The anti-ecclesiastical dimension of the modern cremation movement was understood as suggesting that resurrection was unlikely so the mode of disposition was irrelevant, supporting the popular notion that cremation interfered with resurrection.

Unofficial spokesmen for the Roman Catholic church have been much more explicit in their objections on this ground than have official pronouncements. Father Dorsett is an illustration:

> Anything, therefore, which tended to enforce and illustrate this primary and difficult truth [the resurrection of the body] was guarded, and any-

[12] "Cremation," *The Encyclopaedia Britannica*, VII (11th ed.; 1911), 403.

thing which tended to weaken its hold on the minds of men was discountenanced. . . . If belief in the resurrection of the body is to hold its own in the minds of men we must treat the body in such a way as to impress upon their imagination a picture which shall represent preservation and not complete destruction. Such assistance would not be given with the practice of the columbarium. Thus, on psychological grounds, cremation tends to subvert the belief of men in the resurrection of the body.[13]

It is interesting to note that if such were the case, mummification in the style of the Egyptians would be the ideal Christian mode of disposition of the body.

Unofficial Roman Catholic opposition to cremation has also included the practical argument that cremation destroys evidence of the cause of death by making exhumation and examination impossible. Thus it might abet crime by covering up foul play in the death of the individual.

The position of the Roman Catholic church in the early phases of the modern cremation movement was primarily defensive, feeling it to be a challenge from anti-ecclesiastical forces. The reactions in the interdictions of 1886 showed that this was a disciplinary rather than a theological concern. The defensiveness is further reflected in the following statement in *The Catholic Encyclopedia* of 1908:

It must be remembered that there is nothing directly opposed to any dogma of the Church in the practice of cremation, and that, if ever the leaders of this sinister movement so far controlled the governments of the world as to make this custom universal, it would not be a lapse in the faith confided to her were she obliged to conform.[14]

[13] *Loc. cit.*
[14] IV, 483.

Because in the official position of the Roman Catholic church resistance to cremation is not based on divine law or dogma but only on the disciplinary law of the church, it can be changed by the Pope to adapt to changing circumstances. Exceptions have been permitted.

> The Holy Office instruction on the 10th June 1926, while deploring "this barbarous practice which is contrary not only to Christian but even to natural respect for the bodies of the deceased and wholly averse to the constant discipline of the church from earliest times" was careful to add that "cremation of bodies since it is not wrong in itself may be permitted in certain extraordinary circumstances for grave and certain reasons connected with public welfare."[15]

A more recent illustration of this willingness to grant dispensation is seen in the Roman Catholic church in Japan. Because of the need for usable land in this crowded nation cremation has virtually replaced burial and has been made compulsory in many locations. The Roman Catholic church has allowed its members to be cremated and has even permitted its priests to conduct the burial office at the crematorium.

As the reasons for defensiveness decreased, other relaxations of the rule were apparently made in various places. It is reported that, in 1935, 2624 or forty-six per cent of the cremations in Czechoslovakia were of Roman Catholics.[16] Another indication of the more permissive attitude is the statement of John W. Bieri, S.J., Student Counselor at the Cardinal Stritch School of Nursing, Loyola University of Chicago: "The disposition of the body by burning in the medical schools [after dissection] is not contrary to the law of the church."[17]

[15] Dorsett, op. cit., p. 19.

[16] Wilson and Levy, op. cit., p. 187.

[17] Quoted in A Manual for Simple Burial (Burnsville, N. C.: The Celo Press, 1964), p. 53.

As the movement for *aggiornamento* came to the fore in the Second Vatican Council, petitions were sent from the advocates of cremation requesting that the opposition of the Roman Catholic church to cremation be reconsidered and modified. The Council did instruct that the burial office be restudied and in a papal decree of May 8, 1963 revisions to the canon law were made by Pope Paul VI.[18] This "Instruction with regard to the Cremation of Bodies" acknowledges that where once cremation was an attack against the tradition of the church and an effort to deny the Christian teachings concerning the resurrection of the dead and the immortality of the soul, cremation is today advanced for reasons of health, economy or of public or private welfare rather than out of disdain for the church. So the position of the Roman Catholic church is defined through the following prescriptions:

1. The Christian community is urged to devoutly preserve the practice of burial and to abstain from cremation unless compelled by necessity.

2. Some earlier canon laws should be softened so that the necessity of dispensations should not become more frequent. So Canon 1203, paragraph two (see page 76) about not carrying out an order for cremation and Canon 1240, paragraph one about denying a church burial for those who may have ordered their own bodies to be cremated, should no longer be universally applied. These restrictions should be applicable only when cremation has been chosen out of a denial of Christian teachings or be-

---

[18] Cf. *"Instructio: De cadaverum crematione,"* Acta SS. Congregationum, ACTA APOSTOLICAE SEDIS. (Vatican, 1964), Annus LVI, Series III, Vol. VI, pp. 822–23.

cause of a sectarian spirit or from dislike of the Catholic religion.

3. The sacraments and public intercession should not be denied those who have elected cremation unless the choice was made for reasons indicated above.

4. So that it is clearly evident that the mind of the church is alien to cremation, the rites of church burial and the subsequent intercessions will never be allowed to be conducted in the place of cremation itself, not even by escorting the body to the crematorium.

It is reported that an exception to this last instruction is made in Japan where, because of compulsory cremation, priests are allowed to conduct the burial office at the crematorium. In England there have been numerous instances reported where following a Roman Catholic funeral a nonconformist minister is requested by the family to conduct the committal rites at the crematorium because the Roman Catholic priest is forbidden to do so.

This latest official pronouncement, in the form of an instruction to the bishops of the church, leaves little question about the continued resistance to cremation in principle, but it does remove some of the penalties formerly levied against those of the church who preferred to be cremated. There is little basis at present for an expectation that cremation will be widely employed by Roman Catholics until further modifications are made in their church's teaching and canon law. The possible exception to this is found in countries where cremation is almost universally practiced, such as in Japan, India, Burma and Ceylon.

THE PROTESTANT POSITION ON CREMATION

Because of the great variety of Protestant churches it is impossible to describe an authoritative Protestant position. We can, however, trace the history of some reasonably characteristic Protestant reactions to cremation and point to a consensus that appears to have emerged in the present time.

The Protestant Reformation brought no great change in the practice of burial. The Continental Reformation did not make sweeping changes in the understanding of death and the assumptions about life after death, except for teaching about purgatory and intercessory prayers for the dead. In England there were only minor modifications from Roman Catholic practices in the funeral. Some periods of the Scottish Reformation became so antiritualistic that the corpse was interred with no funeral service at all. But in no instance was there a departure from the practice of burying the dead.

When the modern cremation movement developed, there were elements in it that were antifuneral. An 1886 issue of *The Modern Crematist*, published by leaders of the Lancaster [Pa.] Cremation and Funeral Reform Society, contains this statement:

> How much better it would be if, after the death of a member of the household, no one were to enter therein without a summons from the bereft; if the living could be permitted to vent their grief unchecked by the presence of others; if there need be no preparations for a funeral ceremony and a solemn and awe-inspiring gathering of sad-faced people to remind one, all over again, of the terrible loss one has sustained.[19]

The reaction of the Protestant church to the first cremations of the modern period was largely negative. The Anglican Bishop of Rochester refused the request for

[19] *The Modern Crematist*, I, No. 2 (1886), 22.

permission to erect the first crematorium in England on a cemetery under his jurisdiction. When the English Cremation Society performed its initial cremation at Woking in 1885, there could be no publicly offered Christian prayer, so strong was the opposition of the church. Soon, however, public request for religious service at the time of cremation led to erection of a hall in which religious services could be held.

Most of the arguments advanced by Protestant churchmen were very similar to those of the Roman Catholics.

It was argued that cremation was a pagan custom and thus antithetical to Christian practice. This argument was rather effectively countered by the advocates of cremation who pointed out that burial was also pre-Christian and of pagan origin.

Other churchmen opposed cremation because they found no biblical warrant for it. Even though occasional mention is made of the practice in scripture, as the ultimate rule of faith and practice it offered no injunction to dispose of the dead by cremation. Burial was further supported by the precedent established in the burial of Jesus Christ, if one saw this as normative rather than as just the existing custom of the Palestinian Jews.

Major objection to cremation was based on the doctrine of the resurrection of the body. Taking this concept very literally, some felt that if the body were burned, the resurrection would be prevented. Of course, it was readily pointed out by the supporters of cremation that this was a misunderstanding of the doctrine of resurrection because in the words of St. Paul, "flesh and blood cannot inherit the kingdom of God" (I Cor. 15:50). Furthermore, it was pointed out that dissolution by fire was faster but no more complete than dissolution in the grave.

Advocates of cremation in many instances opposed the notion of merely discarding the dead body and urged that cremation be understood as a thoroughly dignified mode of disposition. The Rt. Rev. R. W. Stannard, Dean of Rochester, speaking for the position of the Church of England, said, "How important then from the Christian standpoint that the disposal of human remains should be attended with the greatest care and reverence, and there can be no cleaner and more beautiful method than that of cremation."[20]

There is no clear historical point at which opposition in the Protestant churches to cremation changed to acceptance. From the early years of the modern cremation movement some Protestant clergymen were active and vocal supporters of the practice. As the Protestant churches gradually became more liberal there was wider acceptance of this mode of disposition.

At present, very few churches are categorically opposed to it. These are likely to be at the conservative end of the Protestant belief continuum. They argue that there is no biblical basis for cremation and that its pagan origins make it unacceptable for Christians.

> The disposal of the body by cremation has in recent years been largely the choice of unbelievers and notorious characters. It is true that some good-living people have requested it, but you will agree that the vast majority have been questionable characters. Such men requested cremation as Josef Stalin, although in his case it was not carried out, Adolf Hitler, Andrei Y. Vishinski, Adolf Eichmann and nearly all of the notorious criminals of our day. There is a great deal of evidence that cremation is not usually the choice of the scripturally enlightened or moral-living individual.[21]

[20] "The Church and Cremation," *Pharos*, XXV, No. 4 (1959), 9.
[21] James W. Fraser, *Cremation: Is It Christian?* (Neptune, N. J.: Loizeaux Bros., 1965), p. 25.

Next to these comes a small group of churches which do not forbid but nevertheless disapprove of the practice.

In the broad center of the continuum are the majority of Protestant churches which accept cremation when it is the preference of the parishioner. They make whatever adaptation in their ritual and practice is necessary to adjust to the differences between cremation and burial. The Church of England, for example, has completely dropped its early opposition and asks now only that cremation take place in the context of the burial office conducted by an Anglican clergyman and that the ashes be deposited in consecrated ground. In fact, Anglican bishops at present commonly participate in the dedications of new municipal crematoriums in England.

At the liberal end of the Protestant continuum one finds active support for cremation as the preferred means of disposition and a growing use of the practice.

The various Orthodox churches fall closer to the Roman Catholic than to the Protestant position. The Greek Orthodox church strongly opposes cremation. The Russian and Armenian Orthodox churches neither prohibit nor approve although in given instances the clergy may refuse to participate actively in rites for the deceased person whose body is to be cremated.

It seems reasonable to say that for the majority of Protestant Christians in the Western world the old theological objections to cremation are now regarded as irrelevant. Churches permit individual members the right to reach their own decisions in the matter. The support of a number of Protestant clergymen in the United States is based less on theological issues than on the possible economies and simplifications which can be achieved through cremation.

THE JEWISH POSITION ON CREMATION

We have already described in chapter one the ancient Hebrew culture's reaction to cremation. In the scriptures there is mention of exceptional cremations after battle or in time of plague or for criminals, but there is nothing that can be interpreted as approval of the practice. There is no explicit or clear law forbidding cremation, but the precedent is clearly established for the practice of burial.[22]

> No reference to cremation is found in the Talmud. However, The Shulhan 'Aruk (Yoreh De'ah, 362) contains the statement, "Burial in the earth is a positive command," a position assumed also by Maimonides ("*Sefer ha-Mizwot*," p. 261). This command is merely deduced from "Thou shalt surely bury him" in Deut. 21:23.[23]

This fifteenth-century interpretation by Rabbi Joseph Garo is obviously based upon an arbitrarily selected emphasis on the word "bury" rather than on the intention of forbidding the dishonoring of the body of an executed criminal by leaving it unburied. However, this compilation of religious rules is regarded as authoritative by Orthodox Jews.

Against this background we must make a distinction between Orthodox and Conservative Judaism and Reform Judaism. The Orthodox and Conservative faiths resist the practice of cremation. They rest heavily upon fidelity to the ancient customs, the scriptural precedents and the talmudic interpretations.

Orthodox Jews regard cremation as unlawful and consider burial as legally required. They do not allow cre-

---

[22] Cf. Gen. 23:19, 35:8; Deut. 21:23, 28:6; I Kings 11:15, 23:22; Ezek. 39:15.

[23] "Cremation," *The Jewish Encyclopedia*, IV (1903), 343.

mated remains to be interred in Jewish cemeteries. Cremation is interpreted by some as mutilation of the body, which is regarded as unlawful. ". . . in the Talmud (Ab. Zarah, I, 3) we find, among other references, the striking statement that 'every death which is accompanied by burning is looked upon as idolatry.' "[24]

The Orthodox position was not easy to maintain once the modern cremation movement developed support. Rabbi Meyer Lerner, whose work *Hagye Olam* (Berlin: 1905) is a definitive statement of Orthodox resistance to cremation, comments:

> I know that in these enlightened lands, for every rabbi who forbids the burial of ashes in the Jewish cemetery, it is easy to find many rabbis who are lenient in this regard and not only among those teachers who deny the written or the oral law, but also among those who still hold firm to the foundations of the Holy Torah, for it is easy to say, "It is permitted," to all those things which most of the people desire.[25]

More liberal Jews (Reform Jews in America and Progressive Jews in England) have accepted cremation as a legitimate practice. They regard the precedent of earth burial in the scriptures as a description of established custom in ancient times but do not vest it with the normative quality of revealed truth. Cremation and burial are regarded as equally acceptable.

The Jewish Encyclopedia notes that various leading rabbis at the turn of the century were either open supporters of cremation or charitably disposed to co-operate with those who wished cremation. "In 1892 the Central

[24] Jakob J. Kokotek, "The Jewish Attitude toward Cremation," *Pharos,* XXVIII, No. 4 (1962), 3.

[25] Quoted by Solomon B. Freehof in *Reform Jewish Practice and Its Rabbinic Backgrounds* (Cincinnati: Hebrew Union College Press, 1944), p. 135.

Conference of American Rabbis resolved 'that in case we should be invited to officiate as ministers of religion at the cremation of a departed coreligionist, we ought not to refuse on the plea that cremation is anti-Jewish or irreligious.' "[26]

Freehof argues that cremation could not have been totally rejected by Jews in earlier times because in the Midrash Vayosha (Jellinek Bet ha-midrash, I, 37) there is a story about the intended sacrifice of Isaac. The interpreter has Isaac say, "I plead with thee, O father . . . burn me well and take my ashes to Sarah, my mother, that she may place it in an urn in her room. . . ."[27]

In sum, the acceptance of cremation by liberal Judaism is based on several points. There is no biblical prohibition of cremation even though burial was clearly the customary practice of the ancient Hebrews. Burial is regarded as a way of respecting the human body and protecting it from desecration or indignity, a purpose served equally well by cremation. The Jewish laws which have been interpreted to make burial mandatory are seen as derived from traditional interpretations rather than from clear statements in scripture.

So we see that in all of the major Western faith groups there has been a parallel pattern. At first there was strong, virtually unanimous reaction against cremation as foreign to Judeo-Christian tradition and practice. In time the early objections tended to be modified and the resistance relaxed. In some instances this relaxation was only in slight degree; in others the moderation of attitude was almost a total reversal of a prior position.

[26] *Loc. cit.*
[27] Freehof, *op. cit.*, p. 134.

V

Legal
Considerations

THERE are several legal or quasi-legal issues involved in the cremation process. These include the legal authorization or consent for cremation, the disposition of the ashes and protection against the destruction of evidence of the cause of death. Before examining these issues, it will be helpful to survey briefly the background of legal regulation of cremation in England and the United States.

We noted in the historical development of the modern cremation movement that the first efforts to cremate in England were met with strong opposition from the Home Secretary. For some years, as a result of the Price decision, cremation was not regarded as illegal but there was no law governing it. A proposed Act of Parliament failed to get necessary support in 1884. Cremations were carried out for more than a quarter-century under regulations voluntarily assumed by the Cremation Society.

In 1902 there was passed an Act of Parliament "For the Regulation of the Burning of Human Remains and to Enable Burial Authorities to Establish Crematoria." Regulations were then published by the Home Secretary in 1903. Among the many provisions of the Cremation Act of 1902 were these: municipal burial authorities were permitted to erect and operate crematoriums; the site of crematoriums was defined and regulated; provisions for state inspection of crematorium facilities were set down; penalties were established for seeking or granting improper authorization for cremation. In 1930, the Home Secretary, following the voluntary procedures adopted decades before, issued regulations prescribing detailed medical certification of the cause of death for bodies to be cremated.

A new cremation act was passed in 1952 which brought the law up to date, although the cause of death certification remained a complex process.

The situation is quite different in the United States where laws dealing with certification of the cause of death and permission to dispose of the body are passed by the individual states. No uniform vital statistics law is in effect, so there is considerable variation from state to state. The diffuse picture is further complicated by the fact that in many states laws dealing with cremation are not separate statutes but are parts of burial, funeral director and cemetery regulative legislation. This makes it extremely difficult to get a broad national survey of all legal regulations of cremation.

CONSENT TO CREMATE

It is sometimes assumed that cremation is possible only if the deceased has left specific instruction regarding the disposition of his body in this manner. Such is the case in the Netherlands, but in both England and the United States written or oral instruction is not required.

According to common law, there is no recognition of any property in the dead body of a human being. By statutory exception, only when there is the intention of bequeathing one's body or parts of it for anatomic research or medical treatment is the condition binding.

In England the cremation act forbids cremation only if the deceased left known written directions that he should not be cremated. In all other instances the application for cremation is filed at the discretion of the executor or next of kin.

In England there is no provision in the law to enforce compliance with the request of a person to be cremated. In spite of written directions to the contrary, an executor could still order burial rather than cremation. In days before cremation was widely accepted practice, it was possible for a person to seek to assure compliance with his wishes by making any bequest to his executor or family contingent upon adherence to his wish to be cremated.

The English form applying for cremation specifically asks whether or not all members of the family have been informed of the application and what their attitude is toward it. However, the executor still has authority to make the application.

In the United States also the body of the deceased is regarded as being in the custody of the executor or next of kin. The elaborate system of application for cremation used in England is not found here. The way in which the body is disposed of is solely at the discretion of the legal custodian. Written or oral instructions to be cremated or not to be cremated are advisory but are not binding. It is not uncommon that some instructions have been left in a will, but that testament was not read until after the funeral had been completed. Thus, those who wish to advise their executors should be certain that the instructions are known and understood.

In the United States only a few states require a special

permit for cremation.[1] Most often the regular burial permit is issued. Some states require that the method of disposal be indicated.

In addition to the burial or cremation permit which is secured by the funeral director, the crematorium requires a signed authorization from the executor or next of kin. This authorization also usually includes instruction for disposition of the ashes or for shipping them to some other community. Some crematoriums are insured against litigation rising out of a charge of performing a cremation with improper authorization. Sometimes when it is impossible to secure all of the necessary signatures for authorizing cremation, an affidavit attesting to the desire of the deceased to be cremated supports the authorization. Crematoriums rightly pay careful attention to securing and recording the proper authorizations.

REGULATION OF DISPOSITION OF ASHES

Most states have legal requirements for the burial of bodies of the dead. Because of the possible dangers to public health, burials are limited to sites designated as cemeteries.

Because there are no appreciable risks to public health from cremated remains, this kind of regulation does not necessarily pertain to the disposition of ashes. In most states one can inurn, inter or scatter cremation ashes so long as he does not create an offense to anyone or violate another's property rights.

No state has specific regulation of the way in which ashes should be inurned or interred. The type of container used is not regulated and in only a few instances is it specified that ashes be placed in a cemetery or columbarium.

[1] Cf. Raymond L. Brennan, "The Burial Permit," *Cemetery Legal Compass,* XVIII, No. 1 (1953), 825.

The legal issue in disposition of ashes has to do largely with the practice of strewing. In part through the efforts of cemetery and columbarium interests, legislation has been passed in California, Washington and Nevada prohibiting the scattering of ashes. The National Park Service also forbids the strewing of ashes in the national parks because of the possible creation of a public nuisance. In 1965 California permitted strewing beyond the three-mile limit at sea and from an airplane flying at more than 5000 feet over non-populous areas. It is interesting to note that these legal restrictions exist in the area of the United States where nearly half of all of the cremations in the nation take place.

There are also some states which have regulations governing the shipping of cremated remains, making it necessary to secure a permit for the removal of the ashes to another state. This again appears to be a carry-over from regulations dealing with the transporting of a dead body. Usually such details are cared for by the funeral director with no necessary involvement on the part of the family of the deceased.

In England there are no laws regulating the means of disposing of the ashes because the law regards the body as disposed of when it is cremated.

PROTECTION AGAINST DESTRUCTION OF EVIDENCE

One of the persistent objections to cremation has been that by burning the body one may destroy evidence of foul play. The assumption is that homicide is encouraged by providing a possible means for concealing the crime. If a body exists, there is the possibility of exhumation and examination even for some period following death. This is a legitimate argument, and cremation advocates have sought to protect against the destruction of evidence.

The voluntarily accepted conditions established by the Cremation Society in England became the basis for legal protection against destruction of evidence of criminal cause of death. In England each cremation authority has a medical referee who authorizes all cremations, but only after there have been independent reports from two medical examiners who must agree regarding the cause of death and must indicate that they find no reason for further examination or autopsy. It must be ruled out that death was caused by poison, violence, an illegal operation, privation or neglect. In the event of violent or sudden death without medical attendance the normal procedures for a coroner's inquest are also required. Cremation is not permitted before the death is registered and it is illegal to cremate human remains which have not been identified. In order to make sure that the medical referee is not circumvented, cremation can be legally carried out only by crematoriums approved by the state, and private cremation is forbidden.

British cremation advocates are dissatisfied with the extensiveness of these requirements.

> Despite the statistical evidence, in the eyes of the Law, burial is still considerably more equal than cremation, for whilst burial is carried out with the barest minimum of [legal] formality and a pathetic lack of elementary safeguard, cremation remains shackled by the taboos and restrictions which reflect the legislative inhibitions of a past age. . . . Britain, the foremost country in the world so far as regards the adoption of cremation, is yet the only country in which the law demands the evidence of two medical practitioners and the final approval of a third before cremation may proceed.[2]

There is also concern in England for the cost of the several medical examinations required by the law. In

[2] "Editorial Comment," *Pharos*, XXVII, No. 2 (1961), 2.

many instances the medical fees amount to half as much as the cremation fees. The Cremation Society holds that the rigid requirements are no longer necessary, especially since they have never been required for earth burials.

In the United States the problem of destruction of evidence has also been seriously regarded. Early advocates of cremation proposed that careful inquests be held for every death in which there was any question about the cause of death.

In all states the law provides for certification of the cause of death by a licensed physician, regardless of the mode of disposition of the corpse. If the person has not been under a doctor's care or if there is a question of death by violence, a coroner's verdict of cause of death is required.

In many states the same permit is used for either burial or cremation, although the mode of disposition is indicated. This permit is not issued until the death certificate is complete. Thus the cause of death is established before cremation is permitted.

In several states special permits for cremation are required. In some few instances a coroner's or medical examiner's approval is required for the cremation permit. In several states cremation may not take place for forty-eight hours following death, unless a health officer orders immediate cremation in the case of contagious disease. If there is question regarding the circumstances surrounding the death of the individual, in some states cremation is not permitted at that time.

Unlike England, the United States does not license crematoriums. All states require that a permit be obtained prior to the cremation. Some states require that a portion of the purchase price of niches and burial plots be placed in trust for the perpetual care of the property.

NOTE: This description of the legal regulation of cremation in the United States has necessarily been general and nonspecific. Because any laws regarding cremation are passed by the states and are often included in a number of acts dealing with death and burial registrations, cemetery regulations, etc., it is virtually impossible to maintain an accurate current digest of the status of all legal regulations in every state. Because of the constant revision of such laws, we have in most instances not named the particular states in which they have been applicable. By pointing to the major issues with which legal regulation is concerned, we have suggested the kinds of questions that need to be clarified in the state in which one resides.

VI

Pastoral
Concerns With
Cremation

WHEN we speak of pastoral concerns here, we are thinking of the ministry of the entire church. This includes the pastoral ministrations of the ordained minister of the congregation, but it is not confined to that narrow boundary. The entire congregation, every member, is more and more involved in doing the work of the church.

When death occurs, the entire church ministers out of concern for the bereaved and their needs. This has been discussed in detail elsewhere.[1] Here we are considering the particular concerns that are related to any special circumstances growing out of the cremation of the body of the deceased.

As we have already seen, in the past the involvement of the church with cremation has been largely defensive. In recent decades, particularly in Protestantism, there has been the evolution of a more sympathetic and co-

---

[1] Cf. Paul E. Irion, *The Funeral and the Mourners* (Nashville: Abingdon Press, 1954) and *The Funeral: Vestige or Value?* (Nashville: Abingdon Press, 1966).

operative position. At the same time there has been developing a broader understanding of the church's total ministry to the whole man, recognizing that the church's concern and service will have many dimensions. Thus the attention of the church is not strictly limited to clarification of the doctrine of the resurrection *vis-à-vis* cremation or to efforts to preserve traditional patterns but also involves an interest in the psychological, social and economic well-being of the bereaved persons.

To organize this discussion we shall consider the church's pastoral ministry relating to cremation in three phases: at the time of planning and decision; at the time of bereavement; in the more extended period of readjustment after loss.

THE CHURCH'S PASTORAL MINISTRY AT THE TIME OF PLANNING AND DECISION

More and more one sees churches taking the initiative in encouraging consideration of cremation. Local congregations are issuing statements regarding funeral practices and their meaning. Such statements very often include a few sentences endorsing cremation as a suitable means of disposition of the body, although not urging it as the normative procedure.

It is not necessary for the church to be involved in special pleading on behalf of cremation. Unless there are some particular circumstances, such as the problem of land usage in a megalopolitan area, on an objective basis burial and cremation are roughly of equal value.

The object of the church's pastoral ministry is to assure that as many options as possible are available to its people. Its concern should be that people of the church have maximum freedom for reasonable choice of those funeral practices which will best meet their needs. Perhaps because of the long history of opposition to cremation in the church, there needs to be a special effort at present to make very clear that there is no reason for the church to oppose cremation. Families should have the opportunity to give serious consideration to cremation, even though many of them may decide to retain the more traditional practice of burial.

Congregational Discussion

One of the most helpful things the church can do is to foster careful and thoughtful discussion of contemporary funeral practices. The ceremonial accompaniments of death have for many become sterile and meaningless as the reasons behind current practices have tended to get lost; the criterion of cost is used as a single measuring stick rather than being used together with other psychological, sociological and theological measures of value. These issues need to be talked over.

It is for this reason that it is not wise for one parish merely to adopt a statement that has been worked out in another congregation. Most of the value comes in the development of a statement by all in the congregation who are interested. The public discussion sessions leading up to a statement of conclusions and recommendations will do much to stimulate a responsible and flexible attitude toward many funeral practices.

The literature of pastoral theology in recent years has provided a number of studies[2] which can guide comprehensive and thoughtful discussion of the funeral in the

[2] C. Charles Bachmann, *Ministering to the Grief Sufferer* (Philadelphia: Fortress Press paperback, 1967).

Paul E. Irion, *The Funeral and the Mourners.*

———, *The Funeral: Vestige or Value?*

Edgar N. Jackson, *Understanding Grief* (Nashville: Abingdon Press, 1957).

———, *For the Living* (New York: Channel Press, 1964).

Granger Westberg, *Good Grief* (Philadelphia: Fortress Press paperback, 1962).

parish. Most certainly, such public discussions should be grounded *not* in the personal preferences or prejudices of the leadership but on the best information we have about death, bereavement, mourning, as well as the function of the funeral and related practices.

Cremation would be one of the subjects included in such thorough discussion. Particularly in communities where cremation is little known or rarely utilized should there be a consideration of the reasons pro and con that emerged in the history of the development of the practice. Careful attention should be given to the objections to cremation which may be raised, testing the accuracy of the assumptions behind these objections. Do persons, for example, feel that cremation jeopardizes belief in the resurrection of the body, or do they assume that burning is pagan or disrespectful?

The relative merits of cremation in lieu of burial following the funeral and cremation immediately after death should be examined. The cost of cremation, with and without inurnment, should be compared with the cost of earth burial according to the price structures of the community. The reaction of the community to innovation and nonconformity in funeral practices is also an appropriate subject for discussion.

The function of such discussion is not to promote cremation but merely to assure that it is a viable option for any families faced with the decision. Such discussions also open the possibility for families to consult with a representative of the church when they are making family decisions about funeral practices.

Planning in the Family

There are two kinds of circumstances under which families can give serious consideration to cremation: in family discussion prior to any actual situation of need, or at a time when a member of the family has died and funeral arrangements are being made.

When decisions are being made at some time before a death actually takes place, there is, of course, opportunity for full discussion and deliberation. There is a real advantage because there is no time pressure to influence the decisions formulated. Further information can be sought, if necessary. Everyone in the family who is concerned with the decision can be consulted. Differences of opinion, if they exist, can be talked over and hopefully resolved.

When death has occurred, normally funeral arrangements are completed within a day or two. If there has not been prior discussion of the possibility of cremation, introduction of the idea at this time may pose some very real problems, unless the practice of cremation is well established as an accepted pattern in the community. To undertake an irrevocable process without careful deliberation can possibly produce frustration and regret. Thus it appears to be unwise to make a hasty decision to cremate.

If immediate members of a family are unanimous in their wish that the practice of cremation be adopted at the times of their deaths, the decision is relatively easy. Then it is largely a matter of interpreting their desire to other relatives and friends. While this is not to suggest that friends and relatives must be consulted in advance, it is helpful to the mourners if it is known that arrangements for cremation have been made as a result of family decision. This is true for any major departures from custom.

Advance planning such as this should always be regarded as advisory and tentative. Even though the plan has evolved through careful deliberation, there is never assurance that some special circumstance will not exist at the time death takes place which may make a change in plans desirable.

For example, for some years Al and Dotty Norris had favored cremation. When Al, Jr., became old enough to be involved in the discussion they talked over carefully their plans for cremation with the ashes to be strewn afterward. All were fully agreeable to this plan. Al Norris died very suddenly. Al, Jr., was on a hospital ship in Southeast Asia recovering from wounds he had sustained as a member of the armed forces. His hospitalization made return home for the funeral absolutely impossible. Realizing the difficulty young Al would possibly have in accepting the unexpected death of his father who, when he last saw him, had been in vigorous health, Dotty thought over their family plans for cremation and strewing the ashes. She knew how difficult it was for her to realize that Al was dead, even with the support of seeing his body at the funeral home. She wondered how it would be for her son if there were no sort of tangible vestige. So she decided that she would arrange, at least temporarily, to place Al's ashes in the columbarium, to have some tangible focus for remembering him. When her son returned home they could reach further decisions.

Mourners should not feel obligated to contradict the meeting of their own needs or needs of other significant persons in order to abide by earlier decisions. The changing needs of the living rightly take precedence over the taboo against contradicting the wishes of the dead.

Differences in Opinion

There are other instances in which families are not unanimous in their plans. This poses the serious question of whose wishes shall prevail.

Legally, it is usual that the executor or next of kin

of the deceased has the right to make the decision, although there is often strong moral and social suasion to abide by the wishes of the deceased.

In the Thompkins home Barbara usually took the lead in making plans and executing them. She was alert, sophisticated, very progressive. Earl Thompkins was just the opposite: plodding, colorless, rather insecure. Their marriage was known by close friends to be largely a matter of convenience. They weathered a number of domestic storms through the years. When Barbara died, with typical efficiency she left detailed written directions for her funeral including the wish that her body be cremated. Earl was very much accustomed to doing as Barbara said, even unwillingly, but he found himself strangely troubled by her suggestion of cremation. Because he was pressed to complete funeral arrangements, he sought out a counselor to whom he had turned before when marital problems had become acute. He explained that he wanted to follow Barbara's wishes but that something seemed to be holding him back from making the arrangements. Because of his previous experience with the couple, the counselor saw the possibilities here that Earl could be either resisting doing what Barbara asked because she was no longer in the decision-making position, or that he was so filled with hostility and guilt growing out of their past relationship that he was unconsciously afraid of venting his covert anger by ordering what he might understand as the destruction of his wife. Even though the counselor did not feel he should volunteer such possible interpretations in the very brief period before arrangements had to be made, he did talk in general terms about ways in which deep and as yet unexplored feelings in Earl might have more to say about the decision than the plans of his deceased wife and supported Earl in following his own inclinations to go contrary to the direction.

Not all instances of the absence of unanimity in funeral planning are the same. Sometimes there are broad, clearly defined areas of disagreement. The husband favors cremation, the wife does not. At other times the lack of unanimity is more subtle. There may appear to be agreement on the surface, but the meanings and motivations beneath the surface may be quite at odds. Part of a family may view cremation as a simpler or more economical way than burial, another member of the family may see it as a means for showing that one can be totally indifferent to a person's body because it is his spirit that really counts. Yet another may unconsciously act out aggressive impulses in planning cremation, while still another resists cremation because of guilt feelings stemming from hostile impulses. While it is unlikely that such a conglomeration would exist in a single family, a broad spectrum of constructive or destructive motivations is possible.

When there is disagreement regarding cremation, whether in advance discussion or at a time when death has occurred, several things need to be examined.

First of all, as far as is possible there should be discussion and understanding of the meanings and motivations held by various members of the family. Each needs to face seriously and candidly the question: what does cremation mean *to me?* The objectivity of a third party, a friend of the family or their pastor, may facilitate this process.

Secondly, there needs to be discussion of whose wishes are to prevail. Are the wishes of the deceased to be respected even though his mourners do not concur? Are the plans of his widow to take precedence over the proposals of his grown children? Is one daughter's resistance to cremation to prevail over the support for cremation given by the rest of the family?

Of course, such questions cannot be answered by majority vote or by seniority rights. The only way in which any such situation of dissension can be resolved is by looking closely at the needs of the individuals concerned and by seeking to meet the need that is deepest and most crucial. Unless there are other rifts dividing a family, the problem should be resolved without difficulty.

Mental Reservations

In still other instances the survivor has deep mental reservations regarding cremation. These sometimes do not emerge until the actual need situation arises.

Sam Hardin had for some years been a vocal supporter of cremation. When the subject came up in discussion at church or with friends, he always asserted very positively, "When I die, cremation is what I want." When Sam died not long ago, his wife, Catherine, who had never taken much part in the discussions, found herself facing a dilemma. In spite of the public statements Sam had made and some of the discussions at home, she found that emotionally it was difficult for her to accept cremation. She preferred the course their families had followed for several generations: burial in the Hardin or Simmons family plot in Oak Hill Cemetery. After talking with Sam's aged parents and with her pastor, she decided that she would prefer to have Sam buried in the family plot, because emotionally she was having a difficult time reconciling herself to cremation. She had always inwardly assumed that when the time came her feelings would just go away, but this was not the case. Her love for Sam made her want to abide by his plan, but her own unexpected feelings made it so terribly difficult.

Mental reservation is a form of resistance. Such resistance needs to be understood and carefully considered. The reasons for the person's hesitancy need to be explored. For some people it is just a matter of lacking information or not having thought things through carefully. Discussion with a concerned friend or pastor will help to clarify the issue and dispel the reservation. In other persons the resistance may grow out of deep unconscious feelings which could be explored and resolved only through some form of psychotherapy.

Because of the irrevocable nature of cremation it is probably best to yield to patterns of resistance when they appear. Although this might appear to be an arbitrary discounting of the values of cremation, it is more an acknowledgment that the therapy of mourning will probably be complicated if sincere resistance is overruled by a process that cannot be undone.

These are some aspects of the period of planning and decision. The church as a congregation or through a concerned pastor offers a number of possible ministries to meet the needs of this period.

Ministering in Planning and Decision

One of the major ministries is to see to it that consideration of cremation is thorough and free. This is done through group discussions as well as in individual families. People should be helped to understand several things.

Families need to know that the decision is theirs to make. The church will not intrude upon their freedom by insisting that only a certain practice is acceptable.

Families need to have the correct information. If possible, the church should assist them to find the answers to any questions they have about cremation: the process itself; the facilities and services available to the community; the costs of all elements of the process; the theological, psychological and social issues that are involved. A decision made without as much information as possible is not a free decision.

Families should understand why it is desirable that advance-planning decisions always be regarded as advisory rather than binding. The goal of any planning should be the provision of maximum help to the mourners, rather than the finding of some assurance that the wishes of the deceased have an ironclad guarantee of execution.

The church can help families to interpret their decisions to the larger family circle if this becomes a problem. In the context of freedom of decision which the church can present, people can find the courage to diverge from long-established patterns which they no longer find helpful.

Finally, the church should seek to assure that every individual who has a legitimate concern with family decisions receives due consideration. This means that there must be mutual understanding of the reasons behind both support for and dissent from family plans. The issue must be decided on the basis of the significance of these reasons rather than as the result of a power struggle. It is quite possible that at times the majority may have to yield to the wishes of one person for whom their decision would create real problems.

From these suggestions it appears that the role of the church's ministry is not to be an advocate or an antagonist of any particular practice. Rather it is a guarantor that decisions are reached in freedom, enlightenment and full sensitivity to the needs of all who are legitimately involved.

THE CHURCH'S PASTORAL MINISTRY AT THE TIME OF CREMATION

We shall approach the second phase of the church's ministry in situations involving cremation by reviewing in general some of the ways in which the church provides for the needs of the bereaved. We usually think of five such functions.

Patterns of Ministry to the Bereaved

The first of these is to provide support for those whose foundation relationships are shattered or eroded by death. Death touches us at the very center of our being by disrupting the pattern of relationships from which we draw personal sustenance. The bereaved often confront a terrifying loneliness. Although it would be foolish to assume that the answer is to substitute immediately another relationship for the one which has been lost, the greatest help is given in supporting the person during the long and painful process of adjustment to his loss. This support, this standing by, this witness to the fact of a shared loss is manifested in several ways by the church. The coming of friends and fellow parishioners to the home of the bereaved with tokens of concern—food, flowers, memorial gifts, offers of assistance—is one such way. The gathering of the community for the viewing and for the funeral service of the church is supportive because the bereaved family is not compelled to stand alone. The practices and customs which the church offers in this crisis situation are supportive because the bereaved are not required to face the situation as if it had never been confronted before.

Acceptance is the second provision the church makes for the bereaved. In its simplest form this is illustrated in the kind of deference normally shown to those who mourn. They can express their feelings more than usual, although they are somewhat circumscribed by community expectations. Special kindness and consideration are shown to them as people try to communicate that they understand and in part share some of the pain the mourners feel. Even though mourners may be so numbed by their loss that they find it difficult to relate to others, the church and the community seek to surround them with loving concern and acceptance.

The church also provides resources to help the bereaved to find a resolution of their relationship with the deceased. Death marks the end of the relationship with the deceased as it has been known. Actual presence and meaningful interaction now have to be translated into a relationship that is best characterized as remembrance. This transition is not easy to make. It involves intellectual and emotional acceptance of the reality and the finality of death. The mourner realizes slowly that the only future relationship with the deceased he can contemplate in hope is radically different from anything he has known. His adjustment to the reality of his situation depends on his willingness to accept the fact that the deceased is gone and that it is no longer possible to relate to him except in recollection. Thus Dr. Erich Lindemann, a pioneer in the modern psychological exploration of grief, speaks of "learning to live with memories of the deceased" as a vital part of the mourning process. Through repeated recall of the deceased, the pain lessens and disappears and the transition to a relationship of memory takes place.

Corollary to this is the provision for the mourner to gain insight into his feelings toward the deceased and toward the situation of bereavement in which he finds himself. Mourners are filled with any of a broad range of feelings: sorrow because of loss, love for the deceased, anger toward the deceased, guilt, bitterness, confusion, loneliness, meaninglessness, anxiety. These feelings, which may occur in a variety of combinations, can best be accepted and understood by the mourner within the framework of gracious acceptance in the church. Whether the feelings are negative or positive, the church by its sustained acceptance can encourage the mourner to bring them to the surface, express them and deal with them.

Finally, the church offers its ministry by providing a system of meanings to enable the mourner to understand his circumstances in the largest possible perspective. Bereavement brings to the thoughtful individual the necessity for reflecting on the meaning of life and death in general, as well as his own living and dying. The church through its ministry of teaching and ritual conveys the meanings that have been part of its heritage— the value of the person, the sustenance of divine love, the hope for new life beyond death.

With this very brief overview of the functions of the church's pastoral ministry in bereavement, let us look more specifically at these functions with reference to cremation and special needs it may create in addition to those needs usually present in bereavement.

Support at the Time of Cremation

A special need for support may arise from the radical and complete removal of bodily presence by the cremation process. This is more extreme than the gradual lessening of a sense of bodily presence in earth burial. Thinking of the body of the deceased in the grave is in one sense a partial defense against the tremendous loneliness death can bring. If this is carried to an extreme as a means for maintaining relationship with the deceased, this is not a good thing. Assumptions of continuing presence of the person in the grave can be a sign of morbidity in mourning. But for a very brief time there can be a kind of cushioning in the gradual transition to life without the deceased.

The radical disposition of the body within the span of a few hours, as we shall see shortly, has some very real benefits, but it also accentuates the sense of aloneness which the mourner feels because it symbolizes the total separation of the living and the dead. In the case of cremation immediately following death this is still more acute.

This accentuation of separation causes the mourner to need even more support than is usually the case. Such support is provided through the pastoral ministry of the church in several possible ways. One of these is through the participation of the congregation in the rites leading to cremation (the funeral) or following cremation (the memorial service). The public sharing of this experience with the bereaved can be very supportive. It indicates to the mourners that others are sharing something of their sense of loss, that others join them in affirming the meanings which the church provides for understanding the crisis of death.

There are some special situations in which such support may be particularly necessary. As we have already noted, one of the reasons that commends cremation is the fact that population mobility has meant that in an increasing number of instances persons are dying at a considerable distance from the communities which they once called "home." It is reported that an appreciable number of cremations on the West Coast and in Florida are arranged so that ashes, rather than the body, may be shipped back to a distant hometown for burial.

A similar situation is the return of the ashes of a member of the armed forces who has died far away from his home. The military will arrange cremation if requested to do so by the next of kin. This cremation is often carried out in facilities most accessible to the area in which death occurred. The ashes are then brought back to the serviceman's home in an urn provided by the government according to the same procedures as the return of the serviceman's body for burial.

The church has a special ministry of support in instances such as these. It is quite possible that close relatives will not have had the opportunity to see the deceased for some time before his death. The circumstances eliminate viewing of his body in death as a means for confirming emotionally the reality of his death. Their church will need to be especially alert to this need. One of the best supportive aids is the visitation of friends and fellow parishioners, giving the mourners repeated opportunities to talk about their loss and to find thus additional confirmation of the death.

Above all, the church should not assume that, because mourners are removed from the time and site of death by days and miles, their tasks of adjustment are any less acute. In fact, this remoteness may actually make their reorientation more difficult.

The way in which members of the congregation stand by all those who are bereaved during the acute phase of their period of need, a week or two following death, is yet another means of ministering supportively. Too often this support is limited only to a day or two following death. Many friends call with offers of assistance, gifts of food, tokens of sympathy. There is always the need for this to continue for a period following the funeral. This would be particularly helpful when cremation has been employed, because of the possibility of heightened loneliness.

Acceptance at the Time of Cremation

There are also additional needs for acceptance which may emerge from the practice of cremation. In some communities where cremation is relatively an innovation or in congregations where it is still regarded as a very exceptional practice, the church has a special responsibility to be accepting of nonconformity. It is interesting to note in our time the way the church is recognizing as a significant part of its mission a ministry to the nonconformist.

The first few times families of a congregation carry out their plans to cremate the dead, there may well be criticism or disapproval from those who stand firm upon traditional practice. The church, through its discussions of funeral practices and its public statements on the subject, needs to express its acceptance by making very clear that cremation is a legitimate custom and that there is no reason against its adoption by members of the church. This acceptance should be affirmed by the full and willing co-operation of the church with plans for cremation and by participation of the congregation in the ritual accompaniments of the process.

We have dealt earlier with the motives for planning cremation. The church, probably ministering through its pastor, will convey acceptance and understanding of the motivational patterns which undergird a family's decision to cremate. These would include their negative as well as their positive motives.

Following the principles of all good counseling, one begins with acceptance of the person where he is—his feelings, his motivations. This is not to say that the pastor or the church would necessarily agree, but any helpful relationship proceeds from acceptance. Then follow discussion, clarification and evaluation of the motivating factors, with appropriate revision of action.

Resolving Relationships with the Deceased

The pastoral ministry of the church is also concerned with assisting mourners to use the experience of cremation as an aid in resolving relationships with the deceased. After cremation, that body which was part of the physical matrix of all relationships with the deceased is so completely changed in nature that it is apparent that the mourner's relationship with the deceased must also be radically different. It is obvious that only a relationship of memory can be sustained.

There may be other situations in which cremation becomes a complicating factor in resolving relationship with the deceased. When strong negativity exists, it is possible for cremation to be used as a means to an unhealthy resolution of the relationship: evading the reality of the person's death, or seeking to mitigate guilt by getting the deceased out of the way as quickly and as completely as possible. When cremation (or any funeral practice) becomes a complicating factor in the resolution of relationship with the deceased, there is reason for the church to be concerned.

Insight and Understanding

The way in which this concern is manifested is by assisting the person to insightful understanding of his feelings. This involves a counseling process that is properly a part of the ministry of the church during the extended period of adjustment following cremation. We shall discuss this process in more detail later.

Here it is enough to say that the ministry of the church, carried out by either congregation or pastor, must be sensitive to the broad variety of feelings, motives and responses which are possible. It should not be assumed that everyone will respond in the expected or in the approved way. Too often the church acts upon this naive assumption and thus cuts itself off from usefulness to the person who is different. To illustrate: how can the church minister effectively to the person who has misused cremation as an avenue for evading the reality of death, if the church has unconditionally endorsed cremation? Or how can the church help the person who respectfully disposes of the body of a loved one by cremation, if the church holds that it is always best to conform to established practice?

Providing Meanings

The church has the task of providing for its people meanings to enable them to cope with the crisis of death. Some of these meanings need to be accentuated when cremation is a part of the situation.

The hope for the resurrection of the dead has been the major resource by which the Christian community has sought strength to confront the reality of death. As the early church resisted various interpretations of the nature of man which bisected him into body and spirit, there was a desire to underline the Christian concern for man as a whole being. This caused the church to frame its resurrection hope in terms of the resurrection of the body. There have been periods in the history of Christian thought when this dogma was interpreted in very literal terms, assuming that the very flesh and bone with which this life was lived would be resuscitated.

It was this sort of literal understanding of the hope for the resurrection of the body that furnished the popular mind with an argument against cremation. This vague fear or doubt about thwarting resurrection still tends to be on the fringe of some resistance to cremation.

For people in the church who have arranged for or carried out cremation of the body of a loved one, this kind of "folk-misconception" may easily prove troublesome. If people have not thought this out, the comments or queries of a sincere but misinformed church member may stimulate doubt or regret or even guilt.

Partly this situation is dealt with in advance by the effective education of the church in which popular misconceptions of the church's teaching can be clarified. But at the time of death and cremation the pastor and astute members of the congregation must be alert for potential misunderstandings of this traditional belief. Reassurance can be offered by pointing out that no major branch of the Christian church holds that cremation is wrong because it is counter to the doctrine of the resurrection of the body.

Another dimension of this doctrine is involved in the concern for associating Christian meanings with the process of cremation. The understanding of man in terms of his wholeness has caused Christian teaching to see value in all aspects of human existence. Although there are exceptions in the history of Christian thought, the mainstream has persistently reaffirmed that the material aspects of life are not to be devalued. This means that the body of a person, either in life or in death, is regarded as something worthy of regard and respect.

Individuals have assigned various meanings to cremation. Some have welcomed cremation as a means for destroying the body which after death they regarded as mere refuse. They have espoused the dualistic view which held that the mortal body of man was inferior to his immortal spirit; the spirit was elevated by death, while the body could be discarded as a worthless shell. Others have thought of cremation as a way of showing regard for the body by enabling rapid and clean dissolution rather than subjecting it to the slow process of decomposition in the grave.

In either instance the church has a responsibility to clarify the meaning attached to the human body after death. The mainstream of Christian thought would resist both the assumption that this dead body itself participates in some form of future life, which suggests that it must be preserved as intact as possible, and the notion that the dead body can be treated with total disregard because it is utterly worthless.

There is in life a definite relationship between an individual's body and his personhood. Not only is his body the tangible part of his existence, but it is also the basis for most of life's significant relationships. We know people, we interact with people, not as abstractions, but in terms of a whole, including their physical bodies.

When death occurs, from a practical and functional point of view the human body becomes an inanimate object. But in the minds of those who knew and loved (or hated) the deceased there is imprinted the memory of past relationship with that person in terms of the appearance and action of his body. This imprint is of sufficient strength to make us continue for a brief time to associate the body and the person.

Part of the function of the church in providing meaning for the death crisis is to enable its members to understand the meaning of the person. Christian teaching has persistently affirmed the worth of the living person as a whole, and continues to affirm a personal value after death.

In a sense, it might be understood in this way. When a man dies, in reality his body has no more value than any other inanimate object—any piece of wood or any rock—except in the memory and thoughts of those who knew him. In the reality-structure of their thinking, value is still imputed to his body. This value is demonstrated by the way in which they deal with his body after death.

That portion of Christian funerary practice which has its legitimate focus on the body of the deceased is seeking to testify to the value which is still apprehended in the person of the deceased. The Anglican Church has sought to express it this way:

> The Church of England is satisfied that this method of disposing of the earthly body [i.e., cremation] is not contrary to the Christian Doctrine of the Resurrection and is to be commended as fully acceptable by Christian sentiment. . . . But Christians, taught by their religion to honour the earthly body and to use it only to the glory of God, must be greatly concerned that its committal to destruction, whether by burial or cremation, shall be as seemly and reverent as possible and shall always be accompanied by a religious ceremony.[3]

Most churches could agree fully with that statement. The church has the task of surrounding cremation with ritual appropriate to convey the meaning of the worth of the person. Cremation is thus to be understood as a respectful means for quick reduction of the body into its component elements. Any disregard for the worth of the personhood of the deceased is not inherent in the process of cremation itself but in the attitudes of those who would use it as a way to get rid of the person of the deceased or to show their disregard for his worth, for even that value which is resident only in memory of him.

By making cremation a part of the ritual of the funeral, the church has an opportunity to communicate those meanings related to the worth of the person which encourage thinking of the deceased with regard and respect as one who has lived and died and is remembered.

Explaining Cremation to Children

In connection with this consideration of the pastoral ministry of the church in relating Christian meanings to cremation, we should include a brief parenthetical dis-

[3] *Advice Concerning Cremation as a Part of Christian Burial* (London: SPCK, 1960), p. 3.

cussion of how these meanings can be related to children in families where cremation is employed.

In all teaching there are two basic aspects: the information which is to be transmitted and the attitude with which it is communicated.

The information regarding cremation cannot be separated from the information regarding death. Much depends, of course, upon the age of the child and the extent of the trauma a particular death has brought to him. Naturally, things have to be explained in terms which he can understand and which are responsive to his needs and his questions. Generally it might be said that the following component parts would be the broad content, although not necessarily the precise language by which the information is conveyed.

Death has occurred. This means that a person's body has stopped working. His heart stopped pumping blood, his lungs stopped bringing in air, his eyes stopped seeing, his ears stopped hearing, his brain stopped thinking, his arms and legs stopped moving and working.

After a person dies, his body is again to become part of the earth. For hundreds of years Jewish and Christian people have told the story of the beginnings of the world in which the first man was made out of the earth and have believed that, when a man dies, his body goes back to its original form as a part of the earth.

There are different ways of returning the body to the earth. Sometimes the body is taken to a cemetery and placed in the ground where over a period of time it gradually dissolves and becomes a part of the earth. Sometimes the body is taken to a crematorium and placed in a cremation chamber where it is made very, very hot. Within an hour or so the body is completely dissolved into a kind of dust which is again part of the earth. This dust is either kept in a small container at the cemetery or is mixed in with the earth.

Of course, when we are alive it is hard for us to think about not being the way we are. It is difficult to imagine becoming part of the earth, being placed in the ground or in the cremation chamber. But we remember that after people have died they no longer see nor hear nor think nor feel anything, so we are not concerned that people who have died will in any way be hurt by whatever way is used to return them to the earth.

The attitudes that will be helpful in interpreting cremation to children are poise, honesty and sensitivity. By poise we mean that the adult will have thought through his own position on cremation sufficiently that he will not be hesitant in the face of a child's questions or upset by what sometimes appears as callousness in a child's reflection on death. The adult will be able to deal with the subject and with questions frankly and candidly. It is best to answer only as much as the child's question requires so that his comprehension will not be strained by a surfeit of information.

The adult will also be sensitive to particular needs which may not find direct expression in the child's words. He will be alert for worries or fears that may not emerge explicitly. He will be careful to use language and thought forms that are meaningful to the child at his level of comprehension.

Because the church is one of the few institutions in our society with a concern for the entire family, its pastoral ministry is extended to the child as well as the adult. A significant part of this ministry is to enable persons of every age to understand life's crises.

The Funeral Service and Committal

The final part of the church's pastoral ministry in situations involving cremation is the most obvious: the funeral service or the memorial service. These services of worship, conducted according to the belief and tradition of the congregation which serves the mourners, are designed to help the bereaved in a number of ways.

The funeral is a way of expressing the meanings contained in the faith which assist mourners to understand and to gain perspective on the crisis that death has brought to their existence. It is a gathering of friends and relatives to support the bereaved and to demonstrate that others share something of the loss they are experiencing. It is a means of providing a climate of acceptance in which the mourners can express their authentic feelings in response to their situation. It is a formalized structure which encourages the remembering of the deceased at the same time that the body of the deceased is separated from the community of the living.

When cremation follows the funeral, it is the last noted function that offers opportunity for a particular pastoral ministry to the bereaved. The funeral service itself leads toward a climax, which is the committal of the body of the deceased to its last resting place with prayers for the repose of the whole person. This act, either in burial or in cremation, marks the moment in which the separation of the living and the dead is felt in all of its intensity. In either instance the separation is complete, but the speed of the dissolution of the body in cremation brings a particular emphasis on this fact.

The funeral service requires several adaptations when

there is cremation. The actual modifications of the wording of the service are very simple and can easily be made by the pastor. Here we are more concerned with the necessary modifications in the form of the funeral service.

These adaptations of form come in the service of committal. The church has not been clear about where and when the committal service should be held when there is to be cremation. In some parishes it has become the custom to conclude the funeral at the church or funeral home with a brief committal service. The body is then taken later to the crematorium by the funeral director. This is particularly true in an area where there is no crematorium and the body must be transported to a facility in another community.

Legitimate question can be raised about having the committal service at a time and place remote from the actual commitment of the body to disposition. It easily becomes a somewhat empty formality. For the mourners more casually related to the deceased this is not too important. But for the mourners of the immediate family, the actual function of the committal as the symbol of separation from the deceased in all but memory and the giving over of his body to the processes of dissolution into its natural elements is diluted.

Thus the church, to exercise fully its pastoral ministration, should make every effort to utilize the resources of the funeral service completely. If it is at all possible, the pastor should accompany the family to the crematorium for committal of the body to the cremation chamber just as he would accompany them to the cemetery for committal to the grave. There is a wisdom inherent in the traditional funeral service which moves to the actual separation from the body of the deceased by giving it over to the process of dissolution. To stop short of this climax is to vitiate one of the important functions of the funeral.

The Church of England, which has very thoughtfully adapted its practices to cremation, has wisely prescribed that the burial office shall be followed and that a short committal service be conducted at the crematorium. As cremation becomes more widely used in the United States it will be well for churches to encourage similar committal services rather than the short-circuiting process of tacking on a committal to the funeral service in church or funeral home and regarding the mission of the church as completed.

One of the distinct advantages that cremation offers is that the funeral service need not be held in the late morning or early afternoon as is now the case. The day-time funeral in our time is drastically reducing the extent of participation by the congregation, making the funeral very often nearly a private family affair. The supportive function of the funeral is severely hindered by this trend. It is difficult for most people to be released from their work for funerals, except when death occurs in the immediate family. If funerals could be held in an evening hour, broader participation would be possible. The funeral could then be followed by committal and cremation, which could take place at night, or the next day with a brief appropriate committal service with the family at the crematorium.

It should be pointed out that this may mean some adjustment in the program and schedule of the church. Efforts in some communities to hold evening funeral services have sometimes been complicated by the heavy schedule of evening meetings and activities. Here the church is faced with the task of deciding just where its real pastoral function lies in each individual instance.

126

The Memorial Service After Cremation

The major alternative to the funeral is the memorial service, which is usually held at the convenience of the family at some time after the disposition of the body immediately following death. Such a memorial service could be held after either burial or cremation, although more commonly it is joined to cremation. Quite possibly this is due to the fact that both cremation and memorial services are variations from the traditional funerary patterns and both would thus appeal to the family desiring or willing to innovate.

The church will certainly offer a pastoral ministry when arrangements are made for immediate cremation and a memorial service. The pastor can offer to conduct a brief committal service with members of the immediate family present at the crematorium. His subsequent conduct of the memorial service should not neglect the emphasis on recollection of the deceased. The fact that the body of the one who died is no longer present makes such an emphasis particularly helpful.

Certainly not every family which arranges for immediate cremation and a memorial service is seeking to avoid the reality of death. But the evasive potential of such a pattern is sufficiently common that the pastor should be alert to the possibility and adapt the ministry of the church to the particular needs which stimulate the desire to evade reality. He will avoid making the memorial service a part of the denial process. This can best be done by using the established order for the burial of the dead with only such revisions as are required by the fact that the body is no longer present. Emphasis needs to be given to the fact that in its best expressions the Christian faith encourages the confident confrontation of life's crises, providing the strength to meet them rather than the opportunity to flee from them. Because the memorial service is so often consciously planned as a form of de-emphasizing the negative aspects of death, the church must remain true to its position that life is best lived when both life and death are confronted honestly and realistically. This is not to say that those who are seeking to evade the harsh reality of death should be openly reproved. Because there is a reason behind their desire to evade, the pastoral ministry of the church must be particularly sensitive to their needs. The careful and thoughtful conducting of the memorial service is one way in which such ministry is offered.[4]

THE CHURCH'S PASTORAL MINISTRY FOLLOWING CREMATION

We have already anticipated a good bit of what might be included in this section. We are thinking here specifically of the kinds of ministry that are offered through the continuing support of the congregation and the pastoral counseling offered by the church in the extended period of adjustment following the funeral and cremation. Depending on the person, this period may vary from weeks to months. We err in the assumption that because the public, structured mourning period lasts only a few days beyond the funeral, the needs of the bereaved do not exist beyond that limited time.

Consolidation of Reality

Usually in the post-funeral ministry to the bereaved some further help is given for consolidating the mourner's acceptance of the reality and the finality of death. In the case of cremation, the radical process of dissolution of the body should have helped to confirm these facts. The exception to this would be in those instances in which cremation was misused as a device for minimizing

[4] Cf. Paul E. Irion, *The Funeral: Vestige or Value?*, pp. 211–19 for more detailed discussion of the memorial service.

the reality of death. This is the situation in which an effort, conscious or unconscious, was made to get rid of the dead body in order to obviate the painful reminders which it would stimulate. Such intention is a defense against facing the crisis of death.

So far-reaching is the reality of this crisis that it cannot be successfully evaded. Sooner or later the mourner has to face the facts, unless his neurotic defenses are perpetuated. Once the reality penetrates the defenses the results can be devastating for some, particularly if all the supportive measures normally present during the acute phases of bereavement are no longer operative. Then the pastoral ministry needs to be ready to provide support and to assist with the development of insights growing out of the confrontation with reality.

Transition From Body Presence to Body Absence

Another need in the post-funeral period to which the pastoral ministry of the church should respond is the need to make the transition in thought and response between body presence and body absence. As we have already pointed out, cremation requires that this transition be made rather quickly because the body is reduced to ashes in a brief period.

The way in which these cremated remains are thought of and the ultimate disposition that is made of them point the direction which the pastoral ministry will take for particular mourners. Some mourners may seek to use the ashes as a means for simulating the presence of the deceased. In spite of the radically altered form of the body, it is not unknown for someone to keep the ashes nearby in the home in an effort to retain something of the personal presence of the dead. In this case, cremation is employed because it is the only legal and practical way to keep the remains in the home. The morbidity of such an approach indicates the need to face more realistically the fact that death has terminated relationships as they have been known. The ministry of the church in such a situation is to provide sufficient support and strength for the bereaved so that he can confront and accept his loss realistically.

The inurnment of the ashes and placement in a columbarium or urn garden represents for most families both a means for disposing of the cremated remains and the establishment of a focus for their remembering of the deceased. It can be a helpful means for recognizing the transition from body presence to body absence. A service of committal when the ashes are placed in the niche or are interred helps to reinforce the recollection process, interpreting again the way in which past relationship is terminated with respect and remembrance.

If, however, memorialization of this type becomes a means of holding on to the person in order to try to maintain more of a relationship than just memory, the process is unhealthy. This is unlikely because the person who is intent upon preserving the identity of the deceased in an attempt to continue relationship will probably not choose cremation. Rather, he will elect burial, in which the assumption of the presence of the body of the deceased in the grave offers greater possibilities for assuming that relationship can continue.

When a family arranges for strewing the ashes, this can mean that they are fully prepared for the transition from body presence to body absence. In many circumstances it would indicate progress in the mourning process. The exception would be those instances in which strewing is part of a pattern of wanting to get rid of the deceased and of any recollection of him.

When strewing of the ashes is arranged, one of the

major tangible points of reference for remembering the deceased is removed. An identifiable location in which the bodily remains are placed is not available. For most families this may constitute no problem. Others may later feel this to be a loss and may require special support to undergird the remembering process.

The pastoral ministry of the church can be of help in such situations in several ways. The church can participate in the strewing by leading a second committal service at the time the ashes are scattered, marking the completion of the identifiable existence of the deceased except for the memories of him which are held.

Another way in which some ministry could be rendered is suggested by a practice of the Church of England. It is increasingly the custom to hold annual memorial services in the gardens of remembrance of crematoriums. The fact that several thousand people often will attend such a service indicates something of the values which are received. Here again is an opportunity to reinforce the recollection process without encouraging the perpetuation of morbid attempts at continuing relationship with the deceased.

Yet another way in which the church might serve with regard to the disposition of cremated remains would be for the church to plan its own columbarium and/or garden of remembrance within the property of the church. This would be very much like the old custom of the churchyard in which the solidarity of the Christian community in life and death was symbolized. In ways such as these can the transition from body presence to body absence be assisted.

Pastoral Counseling

Furthermore, a special ministry of pastoral counseling is called for when there are indications of morbid grief reactions or when very strong negative feelings toward the deceased or toward the mourner himself are manifested. For instances of severe responses of this order, the ministry of the church will be to assist in establishing a referral to a competent psychiatrist or psychotherapist. In less extreme responses, the pastor through acceptance and understanding may enable the mourner to discuss his feelings and the responses they elicit. Because of the potency of such feelings, the parishioner should have the initiative in the discussions. There would then be less danger of destroying the defenses of the mourner and jeopardizing helpful insight than if the pastor were to probe or press for discussion of strong negative feelings.

The pastoral ministry to the bereaved is always concerned that the mourner gain insight into his experience and his feelings toward it. This may include his feelings of love and loss, his loneliness and the steps he is taking to meet it, his difficulties in fathoming the meaning of death and why it occurred at this time, his anxieties at the thought of his own death, his possible bitterness produced by tragic circumstances, his ambivalent feelings growing out of thinking back over past relationship with the deceased, possible hostility and guilt, his desires to evade facing the full implications of the situation.

Such pastoral concerns are present in all bereavement. The form which funerary practices take may, to the astute pastor, be an indicator of particular needs. When cremation is arranged, he will be especially alert to indications of those exceptional instances in which the person manifests a need to evade death or feelings toward the deceased. He will note carefully what cremation seems to mean to the mourners and what their motivations appear to have been for completing the arrangement. He will take special note of the feelings surrounding immediate cremation and a subsequent memorial service.

When special needs are detected, the pastor must seek to be available to the mourners through consistent pastoral visits. He will, without violating their privacy with specific description of their need, encourage the support and acceptance which members of the congregation can show toward the bereaved, providing a context in which the mourners will more readily face their own feelings.

To bring comfort to those who mourn has from the beginning been part of the mission of the church. Such comfort is most helpful when it is specifically directed toward individual situations and particular needs. In other studies in recent years there have been helpful directions for ministering to the bereaved based upon the variations of social and psychological needs in each individual mourner. To this most significant variable we have sought here to add another dimension: the variable of the funerary practice which is arranged and carried out in a particular bereavement. This too becomes an important indicator of the needs toward which the pastoral ministry of the church is directed.

Appendix

How Do You
Feel About
Cremation?

AS the practice of cremation becomes a viable option for more and more people, individuals face the task of examining their own attitudes and formulating their own positions on the question. It would be foolish to assume that an objective measure could be devised to enable a person to gauge the extent of his acceptance of or resistance to cremation. Still it may be possible to explore some areas which very often are significant in the development of attitudes toward cremation.

Following are a series of statements to which you can respond "yes" or "no." Record your answers and then we shall discuss briefly the issues involved.

1. Usually I feel quite at ease in new circumstances —a new community, a new job, a new circle of friends.

2. If a child of a family were to die and later the family were to move to another state, they should consider the possibility of moving the grave of the child to their new community or plan to return to that cemetery for interment when other deaths occur in the family.

3. It is disrespectful to think or speak ill of the dead.

4. One of the least helpful parts of American funeral practice is the custom of seeing the body of the deceased.

5. It must be a source of comfort for a bereaved family when a sizable number of friends and relatives attend the funeral.

6. I believe it is comforting to use a burial vault to protect the body from infiltration of water in the grave.

7. If one has the opportunity, it is a moral obligation to visit graves of deceased relatives occasionally.

8. I have sometimes wondered what it "feels like" to be dead.

9. When a new laborsaving device relating to my daily work appears on the market, I can hardly wait to try using it.

10. My family has for several generations buried its dead in a family plot.

11. I believe that it is better not to think about disagreements or arguments one has had with the deceased.

12. It is probably wise for a mourner to take a trip shortly following the funeral because new surroundings and new interests will keep him from dwelling on his loss.

13. In my own experience there have been times when I have genuinely regretted the fact that work or travel prevented me from attending the funeral of a friend or neighbor.

14. When standing at the grave of a famous person,

such as the late President Kennedy, it is very nearly like being in the presence of the person.

15. Modern embalming is helpful since it assures mourners that the body of their loved one will be preserved for a considerable time.

16. A funeral in midwinter always seems to me singularly bleak because one feels particularly bad about putting the casket in the cold, frozen earth.

17. I would not be embarrassed if a discussion revealed that I was the only one in the group who had not read the latest best-seller.

18. It is the custom in our family to visit the graves of close relatives at least several times a year, e.g., on holidays, birthdays, anniversaries.

19. It is a good thing that our human nature tends to cause us to idealize the dead.

20. When I have a serious problem I find that going to a movie or reading a novel helps me to relax and get away from it for a time.

21. It is unfortunate that in many communities people do not feel a responsibility to attend funerals for others than members of their families.

22. I get a different feeling standing at the grave of one who has died recently than I do at the grave of one who has been dead for many years.

23. Keeping some belongings of the deceased helps mourners because this enables them to retain a sense of nearness to the one who has died.

24. I would have real reservations about permitting an autopsy on the body of a loved one unless it

was absolutely necessary because it seems like submitting the person to additional suffering.

The purpose of these statements and your responses to them is not to enable you to establish a certain score on the basis of which it would be decided whether or not you favor cremation. Rather, this has been an attempt to expose you indirectly to eight different issues which seem to have bearing on one's attitude toward cremation. On the basis of your reactions to these issues it is to be hoped that you will have a clearer picture of just how you do feel about cremation.

Willingness to innovate or to be nonconforming (statements 1, 9, 17). An affirmative answer to these statements would indicate that one is open to the possibility of novelty or that one is not overly sensitive to pressure to conform. As we have already indicated, because cremation in many communities is regarded as nonconformity, the supporter of cremation has to be sufficiently secure to be able to vary from established patterns. If a person is not willing to innovate, he will be much more inclined to abide by existing patterns even if he does not particularly favor them.

Importance of a localized focus for remembering the dead (statements 2, 10, 18). A negative response to these statements would imply that an individual does not feel the need for some specific location as a focus for thinking of those who have died. This is not to say that he is averse to remembering the dead. Rather it indicates that he does not need an actual place to focus this recollection. Affirmative responses to these statements would not necessarily show an unfavorable attitude toward cremation but these probably would indicate that scattering of the ashes would not be approved by the person. When considering one's own cremation, it is helpful to inquire into the ways in which one wishes to be remembered. Do I want to be recalled in terms of my deeds, my attitudes, my contribution to family and community, or in terms of my physical body? Such questions help to determine the necessary focus.

Willingness to acknowledge and accept negative feelings toward the deceased (statements 3, 11, 19). Negative responses to these statements would point to a capacity to accept such feelings. On the other hand, affirmation of the statements implies that one feels that it is better to avoid any negative feelings toward the deceased. One who is capable of acknowledging and expressing such feelings will be less likely to utilize cremation as a means for acting out negativity because the channels for expression are open. On the other hand, for one who has the feelings but lacks the capacity for expression there should be careful consideration of the possibility that cremation is an aggressive or guilt-relieving device. This is not to say that this is inevitably the case, but rather that some introspection is in order if strong negative feelings lack other means of expression.

The acceptance of reality (statements 4, 12, 20). "Yes" responses to these statements indicate a desire to evade reality in the death and bereavement situation, while "no" responses point to a willingness to accept reality. The pattern of one's responses here tends to show if a person supports cremation out of a desire to avoid reality or to escape from some of the painfulness of the experience of mourning. The extent to which a person is willing to face the reality of his situation is a very important criterion in determining how helpful cremation will be in his experience of mourning.

The pattern of attendance at funerals (statements 5, 13, 21). This is another way of getting at the patterns of avoidance or confrontation. Positive response to these statements indicates a willingness to confront the situation in terms of participation in the funeral, while negative response implies the likelihood of a desire to evade the situation by nonparticipation. A pattern of evasion or avoidance could quite possibly mean that cremation would be supported as a means for truncating the pattern of funeral practice in order to escape from the situation.

Ways of thinking of the body presence of the one who has died (statements 6, 14, 22). Responding "yes" to these statements points to a way of thinking about the deceased as if he were present as a person in the grave. Negative responses indicate that one does not maintain a strong sense of body presence when thinking of one who has died. One who thinks strongly in terms of body presence will probably be resistive to cremation because the obvious deterioration of the body in the process makes it very difficult to sustain the idea of a presence. One who does not think so strongly in such terms will find cremation more acceptable.

A desire to retain relationship with the deceased (statements 7, 15, 23). Responding affirmatively to these statements possibly indicates that the individual hopes to hold to something of a relationship with the deceased by maintaining a sense of body presence after death. Negative responses to the statements imply a willingness to give up the sense of body presence after death and the disposition of the body, acknowledging that any possible relationship is radically different from anything that has been known. If it is important to a person to hold to the notion that the deceased is still in a way present, cremation will probably not be acceptable because of the drastically altered form of the body in the process of rapid dissolution.

The extent of one's identification with the deceased

(statements 8, 16, 24). It seems almost inevitable that there be something of this identification in us all. The death of another causes us to think, even fleetingly, of our own death. This joining of our death to the death of someone else involves our own bodies, for they will die. If this identification is quite strong, one may tend in imagination to put himself in the place of the deceased. Dread of burial or of cremation under such circumstances may well be a person's resistance to the thought of his own burial or cremation. This lies behind many of the measures which are employed to protect the dead body from indignity, from exposure to the elements or from any physical harm. For one who felt such identification very strongly, cremation would be lacking in appeal. Affirmative responses to the statements would indicate the presence of such identification while negative replies would point to a greater freedom from it. It should be stressed that *unless you yourself are willing to be cremated, there is real basis for questioning the wisdom of having a loved one cremated.*

The intention of this simple device is not to enable a person to total up "yes" and "no" responses and then to decide how he feels about cremation. There is no test to be passed. Rather, this has been an attempt to begin to immerse the reader in some of the issues that are crucial in developing attitudes toward cremation.

Implicit here is the fact that it is undesirable that decisions on such an important matter should be based on rash, hasty judgments. Pervasive attitudes are very much involved in the matter. To ignore these in favor of quick decisions with no forethought or prior discussion seems very unwise. One cannot give a "snap" answer to the question: How do you feel about cremation?

Bibliography

BOOKS

Bachmann, C. Charles. *Ministering to the Grief-Sufferer.* Philadelphia: Fortress Press (paperback), 1967.

One of the more recent treatments of the pastoral care of the bereaved, including helpful sections on the ministry of the funeral.

Basevi, W. H. F. *The Burial of the Dead.* London: George Routledge & Sons, 1920.

A detailed historical, cross-cultural study of burial and cremation from prehistoric times to the twentieth century.

Bendann, Effie. *Death Customs: An Analytical Study of Burial Rites.* New York: Alfred A. Knopf, 1930.

An examination of the funerary practices of many nations and religious groups from early times to the present. Particularly helpful in understanding the relation of these practices to the belief and thought forms of a people.

Bowman, Leroy. *The American Funeral: A Study in Guilt, Extravagance, and Sublimity.* Washington, D.C.: Public Affairs Press, 1959.

The first of the contemporary critiques of the funeral, written from the viewpoint of a social scientist, who sees the funeral as an anachronism in urban mass society. Supports cremation as a way of making the funeral more economical.

Cobb, John Storer. *A Quarter-Century of Cremation in North America*. Boston: Knight & Millet, 1901.

As indicated by its title, a historical sketch of the foundation of cremation societies and of crematoriums during the first decades of the modern cremation movement. Gives good background on the moving forces behind the development of the practice.

Dowd, Quincy L. *Funeral Management and Costs*. Chicago: University of Chicago Press, 1921.

One of the early social scientific studies of the funeral. Contains material on the modern development of cremation and discusses witnessing a cremation.

Erichsen, Hugo, M. D. *The Cremation of the Dead*. Detroit: D. O. Haynes & Co., 1887.

A volume describing the history of cremation, by one of the early ardent supporters of the practice in the United States, the founder of the Cremation Society of America.

Eusebius. *The Church History of Eusebius*. Bk. V, chap. 1, in *Select Library of Nicene and Post-Nicene Fathers*. Ed. Philip Schaff and Henry Wace. New York: Charles Scribner's Sons, 1905. I, 215–17.

An account of the use of cremation as a repressive measure during the early persecutions of the Christian church.

Fraser, James W. *Cremation: Is It Christian?* Neptune, N. J.: Loizeaux Bros., 1965.

A booklet strongly opposing cremation from the

standpoint of conservative evangelical theology and biblical literalism which repeats many of the arguments used against cremation in the nineteenth century.

Freehof, Solomon B. *Reform Jewish Practice and Its Rabbinic Background.* Cincinnati: Hebrew Union College Press, 1944.
A definitive statement on the practices of Reform Judaism with scriptural and talmudic documentation which contains a treatment of cremation from the viewpoint of both Orthodox and Reform traditions.

Habenstein, Robert W. and William M. Lamers. *Funeral Customs the World Over.* Milwaukee: Bulfin Printers, 1960.
The most complete recent work describing in detail the funerary practices of peoples of every region and culture.

————. *The History of American Funeral Directing.* Rev. ed. Milwaukee: Bulfin Printers, 1962.
A detailed study by two sociologists of the development of funeral practice and professional funeral service in America.

Harmer, Ruth M. *The High Cost of Dying.* New York: Collier Books, 1963.
A critique of the contemporary funeral, using an economic criterion, which sees the funeral as lacking in meaning and helpfulness.

Irion, Paul E. *The Funeral and the Mourners.* Nashville: Abingdon Press, 1954.
An effort to make the funeral a significant part of the therapy of mourning by employing the best insights growing out of psychological studies of grief.

————. *The Funeral: Vestige or Value?* Nashville, Abingdon Press, 1966.

Based on religious, cultural, social and psychological understanding of the nature of the funeral. Contemporary practices are evaluated in the light of the valuable functions of the funeral and new designs are proposed to conserve significant values. Has sections on cremation and on the memorial service.

Jackson, Edgar N. *For the Living.* New York: Channel Press, 1964.

A thoughtful, easily read description of ways in which the funeral provides help to the bereaved. Well grounded in psychological and theological understanding.

————. *The Christian Funeral.* New York: Channel Press, 1966.

An analysis of the religious significance of the funeral with special emphasis on the funeral meditation.

James, E. O. *Prehistoric Religion.* London: Thames & Hudson, 1957.

A comprehensive study which shows the close relationship between prehistoric man's religion and the ways in which he met the crisis of death as shown in his funerary customs.

Jones, P. Herbert (ed.) *Cremation in Great Britain.* London: The Pharos Press, 1945.

Contains material on crematoriums in Great Britain, on the cremation laws of England and Scotland, on the history of cremation and on latest developments in the process.

Mandelbaum, David. "Social Uses of Funeral Rites," in

The Meaning of Death. Ed. Herman Feifel. New York: McGraw-Hill, 1959.

The book is a very excellent treatment of many aspects of death and bereavement. This particular chapter provides a helpful understanding of the ways in which cultural anthropology sees funeral customs as meeting the needs of the mourners.

A Manual for Simple Burial. Burnsville, N. C.: The Celo Press, 1964.

A booklet representative of current efforts at funeral reform, suggesting patterns by which through group action funerals may be made simpler and less costly. Sees immediate cremation as a means to that end.

Polson, C. J.; R. P. Brittain; T. K. Marshall. *The Disposal of the Dead.* New York: Philosophical Library, 1953.

A very comprehensive study of burial and cremation practices, particularly those of England. Includes a careful historical survey, excellent descriptive material, as well as a summary of the attitude toward cremation in a number of religious groups.

Rush, Alfred C. *Death and Burial in Christian Antiquity.* Washington, D. C.: The Catholic University of America Press, 1941.

A survey of early Christian attitudes and funerary customs described as supporting the anticremation position of the Roman Catholic church.

Tertullian. *De Resurrectione Carnis,* Vol. XV, cap. vi; and *De Anima,* cap. ix, in *The Writings of Tertullian.* Ed. Alexander Roberts and James Donaldson. Edinburgh: T. & T. Clark, 1870.

Material descriptive of the attitudes favoring burial in the Christian church of the early centuries.

Warner, W. Lloyd. "The City of the Dead," in *Death and Identity*. Ed. Robert Fulton. New York: John Wiley & Sons, 1965.

A chapter describing the symbolic meaning and value of the cemetery in the life of the community and the individual. Particularly helpful in understanding the value of a focus for remembering the deceased.

Wilson, Sir Arnold and Hermann Levy. *Burial Reform and Funeral Costs*. London: Oxford University Press, 1938.

Particularly helpful as a resource for studying the history of cremation in various cultures.

ENCYCLOPEDIAS

"Cremation," *The Catholic Encyclopedia*. IV (1908), 481–83.

A statement of the response of the Roman Catholic church to cremation from early times through the institution of canon law prohibition of cremation in the late nineteenth century.

"Cremation," *The Encyclopaedia Britannica*. 11th Ed. VII (1911), 403–6.

"Cremation," *The Encyclopaedia Britannica*. 14th Ed. VI (1964), 721–22.

Some helpful information regarding the historical development of cremation in various cultures.

"Cremation," *The Jewish Encyclopedia*. IV (1903), 342–44.

A description of the background in scriptural and rabbinical sources for the Jewish attitude on cremation.

"Death and Disposal of the Dead," *Encyclopedia of Religion and Ethics*. Ed. James Hastings. IV (1912), 411–511.

A detailed description of the practice and rationale of funerary customs of all of the great religions of the ancient and modern world.

PAMPHLETS

Advice Concerning Cremation as a Part of Christian Burial. London: SPCK, 1960.
A booklet approved by the Archbishops of Canterbury and York describing in practical fashion the participation of the Church of England in cremation rites.

Bonnell, Henry Houston. *Cremation: Scientifically and Religiously Considered*. Philadelphia: Press of D. C. Chalfant, 1885.
A typical early apologia for cremation, tracing the history of the practice and its values for modern man. By indirection it affords an interesting study of the arguments advanced against cremation in the early modern period.

Cremation . . . The Way of Nature. Education and Information Committee of the Cremation Association of America.
A small pamphlet made available through many crematoriums in the United States answering questions about cremation.

Eighty Years of Cremation in Great Britain (1874–1954). London: The Cremation Society, 1954.
A brief historical survey of the development of cremation in the modern period.

Facts about Cremation. London: The Cremation Society, 1965.

Explains the procedure for arranging cremation and urges membership in the Cremation Society.

A *List of Books, Pamphlets and Articles on Cremation Including the Cremation Association of America Collection.* Chicago: The John Crerar Library, 1918.

This bibliography contains most of the writings on cremation in English, French and German, particularly those of the early modern cremation movement. The Crerar Library has one of the most complete collections of cremation literature in the country.

Manual of Standard Crematory-Columbarium Practices. Interment Association of California, 1941.

A revision and republication by the Cremation Association of America of a portion of a broader document, *Manual of Standard Interment Practices and Standard Crematory-Columbarium Practices.* Provides a statement of recommended policies and procedures for the operation of crematoriums and columbariums.

Proceedings of the Conventions of the Cremation Association of America.

Published annually by the association, containing transcripts of all addresses and business sessions at its conventions.

Why Cremation? London: The Cremation Society.

A brief pamphlet promoting the use of cremation in England.

Periodicals

Holland, P. H. "Burial or Cremation," *The Contemporary Review,* 1878.
   An article denying the necessity of cremation by the medical inspector of burials in England, giving answer to Sir Henry Thompson's article in the same journal initiating the modern emphasis on cremation in England.

The Modern Crematist. Lancaster, Pa.: M. L. Davis & W. U. Hensel, 1886–89.
   One of the first journals strongly advocating cremation. Provides good illustration of the arguments advanced in favor of the practice and the answers given to opponents of it.

National Cremation Magazine. The Cremation Association of America, 1966——.
   The new official publication of the association.

Pharos. London: The Cremation Society, 1934——.
   Official publication of the cremation movement in England and abroad.

Index

Type, 10 on 12 and 9 on 10 Caledonia
Display, Optima and Futura
Paper, White Textbook Antique